THE MASTER ARCHITECT SERIES V

Haigo Shen & Partners

Selected and Current Works

WITHDRAWN

THE MASTER ARCHITECT SERIES V
Haigo Shen & Partners
Selected and Current Works

First published in Australia in 2002
by The Images Publishing Group Pty Ltd
ACN 059 734 431
6 Bastow Place, Mulgrave, Victoria, 3170
Telephone (61 3) 9561 5544 Facsimile (61 3) 9561 4860
Email: books@images.com.au
Website: www.imagespublishinggroup.com.au

National Library of Australia
Cataloguing-in-Publication data

    Haigo Shen.

    Includes index.

    ISBN 1 876907 33 9.

    1. Haigo Shen (Firm). 2. Architecture – Taiwan.
    3. Architects – Taiwan. 4. Architecture, Modern –
    20th century – Taiwan. (Series: Master architect series V.)

720.951249

Edited by Renée Otmar, Otmar Miller Consultancy Pty Ltd, Melbourne

Designed by The Graphic Image Studio Pty Ltd, Mulgrave, Australia

Printed in Hong Kong

Contents

WITHDRAWN

Introduction

WITHDRAWN

Haigo Shen & Partners, The Pioneers of Modern Taiwanese Architecture
by Wu Kwang Ting

By the end of the 19th century, under the leadership of the Ching Imperial Commissioner Liu Ming-chuan, Taiwan had already become an advanced area in a weak and desperate China. It had a new north–south-bound rail system, new electrical systems in major cities, commercial ports along the major rivers, and a very prosperous export trade. Even before the Japanese colonization (1895), Taiwan was already equipped with a modern workforce. Thereafter, during the Japanese occupation, the Japanese carried on the development strategy of Liu Ming-chuan to develop Taiwan into an island of great military and economic strategic value. In other words, because of the island's strategic location, from the time of Liu Ming-chuan's administration until the end of the Japanese occupation (1945), Taiwan's physical construction was never totally "Chinese" or "Japanese." In fact, after the Nationalist Government moved to Taiwan (1949), the island of Taiwan between 1950 and 1960 under the rule of the KMT, was in a state of civil war with uncertainty. After 1960, the war situation between the Taiwan Straits calmed down; nevertheless, the Nationalist Government's policy in the construction of Taiwan has followed the policy of the late Ching government and the Japanese colonial government. It was never intended to fully construct the island's infrastructure; on the contrary, the policy tended to carry on a more practical strategy of economic development. The postwar modernization experience of Taiwan began after 1960. It was during that period that the development of modern architecture began.

In contrast to the social development of Taiwan's modernization experience, Taiwan's architectural development faced two major problems which needed to be overcome: First, the lack of experienced professionals; second, the lack of proper channels for training and re-educating in the acquisition of new professional and technological know-how. During the period 1950–60, in Taiwan all the resources were under the control of the government, and the architectural profession was often neglected. However, owing to the Korean War, after which the United States government had re-kindled the allied relationship with the Nationalist government in Taiwan and, since 1951, had begun to provide first, political and military aid, then for people's daily needs. This was known as the "US Aid Program," which helped to lead Taiwan into the first phase of modernization. With regards to the development of architecture, the military construction under the US Aid Program provided an opportunity for young architectural professionals in Taiwan to help resolve the problems mentioned above. Haigo Shen was one of the young architects who gained his experience during this period and subsequently had a great influence on the modern architectural development in Taiwan. Haigo Shen started his own practice in 1958. Before that he worked in the Continental Engineering Corporation, Chinese Army Combined Service Force General Headquarters and US Military Assistance Advisory Group, ROC. The US Aid Program not only provided political and military help to Taiwan, but also provided opportunities for Taiwan's architects to work with US architectural and engineering professionals who had up-to-date knowledge. It can be said that, partly as the result of US aid, the first generation of Taiwanese architects developed their modern experience.

Haigo Shen was not only an outstanding professional during this process of modernization, he was also a great leader and manager who believed that architecture is the result of team work. His office, Haigo Shen & Partners, was organized in the very beginning as a large office with diversified specialization, which was implemented much earlier than the economic take-off of Taiwan in the 1970s and 1980s, has been maintained until today. In another words, Haigo Shen's vision in recognizing the need of specialization and team work in architectural practice in Taiwan proved his farsighted thinking; his predication in the specific need in the architectural profession was also a very sensitive idea. Under these conditions, the early work of the office, such as Chia Hsin Office Tower (1967), Good Shepherd Church (1967), Chapel of St. John's & St. Mary's Institute (1968), the Customs Office Headquarters (early 1970s), and Terminal Building, Taipei International Airport (1971) are important examples of Taiwan modern architecture in the postwar era of Taiwan. In the above examples we can see that the Chia Hsin Office Tower and the Customs Office Headquarters are typical examples of the self-designed Western-style office building developed out of the Taiwan modern architecture experience. The Shepherd Church, with its red-brick walls and traditional courtyard space layout, reflects the cultural and spatial design issues at that time. The design of Taipai International Airport, in trying to catch the Chinese traditional architectural motif especially in the handling of the detail design, provides a new vision. With the Chapel of St. John's & St. Mary's Institute's mature expression in its structural design, these diversified design thinking and expression provide very good proof of today's modern Taiwan architecture development.

Forty years ago, Haigo Shen's office provided a prediction that is hard to imagine. From this point of view, with Haigo Shen's "prediction," like the Italian Futurist architect Sant'Elia's prediction to the future of cities, and also like the prediction of the Chicago architect Louis Sullivan as to the future of the form of commercial architecture, he seems to have become the most influential city and architecture "story teller" of post-1960s Taiwan.

Haigo Shen & Partners not only developed a diversified teamwork approach internally; they also rigorously sought international architects as "technical partners" to reinforce their sense of mission in promoting the modernization of Taiwanese architecture.

Internationally famous architects who have worked with Haigo Shen Partners (HSP) include HOK, KCMI, Sasaki & Associates, Michael Graves, PCF, RTKL of USA; Kenzo Tange, Neikkei Sekkei of Japan; Wong and Oyang of Hong Kong; and Weathered Howe Pty Ltd of Australia. These experiences make HSP one of the few large architectural firms which could satisfy the needs of the economic development of the '80s in Taiwan. During that period, large-scale architectural works included the Taipei World Trade Center's Exhibition Center (1989, with HOK), the International Convention Center (1989), Taipei Main Station (1989), Grand Hyatt Hotel, Taipei, Taipei Terminal Special District Urban Design and Planning Project (1990, with Sasaki & Associates), and MCTS Transit System and station design (1988–96). These are the architectural works which are considered to be the works of a local architect with a high enough standard to be compared with the works of international architects.

In the late '90s and early 2000s, the Museum of Prehistory (2001, with Michael Graves) and the Museum of Marine Biology & Aquarium, (2000, with KCMI) are good examples of HSP's works, the results of close collaboration with international architects. These works have gained praise for their high design quality, and have influenced and elevated the architectural professional standard. HSP's latest works in collaboration, such as the President International Tower, located in the Hsin-Yi planning district (2003, with Kenzo Tange), the Taishin International Bank Tower at the Jen-I Circle (2004, with PCF, I.M. Pei's partnership office) are designed with a new vision which will no doubt change the skyline of Taipei City. HSP's mission in city and architectural development is not only confined to Taipei. The company has equally impressive works in Kaohsiung and throughout Taiwan. In 2001, HSP participated in the international competition for the planning of the 2008 Olympic Sports Center and National Exhibition Center in Beijing, in collaboration with the Architectural Design Institute of the Ministry of Construction, People's Republic of China, and Great Earth Architects (International), Beijing. The entry has won a citation for its excellence of design, providing the opportunity for HSP to join other international architects in the development and construction of Beijing.

HSP also possesses an impressive body of work in campus planning in Taiwan. Its design of Taipei American School (1987–90), the Main Library of National Taiwan University (1998), the Campus planning of Chung-Cheng University and its Classroom Complex (1991) and Auditorium (1994), and the Library and Information Center of National Chia-Yi University are excellent examples of HSP's involvement in the process of improving the quality of the environment of higher education.

In conclusion, from my own point of view as a person who, for a long time has been engaged in the research of the architectural development of Taiwan, HSP's works in architecture and planning have had a positive impact on the development of modern architecture in the postwar era. It touched me that Haigo Shen established the Haigo Shen Architectural Education Foundation in 1998 in order to donate his income to help to elevate the architectural professional standards in Taiwan and China by providing scholarships, research and traveling grants to young and promising professionals.

As we all know, it is impossible to be rich under the current circumstances of architectural practice in Taiwan; however, Haigo Shen's efforts to establish a foundation in helping young architects have no doubt stirred fresh air in this cold architectural professional society and in the end they will be important notes in Taiwan's modern architectural history.

Education

Main Library, National Taiwan University

Design/Completion 1989/1998
Taipei, Taiwan
National Taiwan University
35,472 square meters
Reinforced concrete
Gables, arched windows, arcades and ornaments, and a special glazed tile

Creating a terminal focus for the central axis of the National Taiwan University campus, the new Main Library is a pivot in the overall campus plan. It responds to particular site conditions, presenting a strongly symmetrical façade to terminate the central boulevard and developing an open courtyard next to the student activity center, which also lets in natural light to the lower level of the library. The rich vocabulary of projections and indentations, arcades and arched openings, links the new building to the traditional architecture of the campus, and expresses the development of the many functions within.

The interior was designed with the advanced systems of information storage and retrieval, multi-media access and computer access. Not only are there mechanized shelving units, but the rare book collection is housed in cases custom designed for the preservation of historic materials. Further embodying the way in which the new library continues traditions of National Taiwan University, the antique study tables, used by generations of students in the reading room of the old general library, were carefully refinished for use in the new facility.

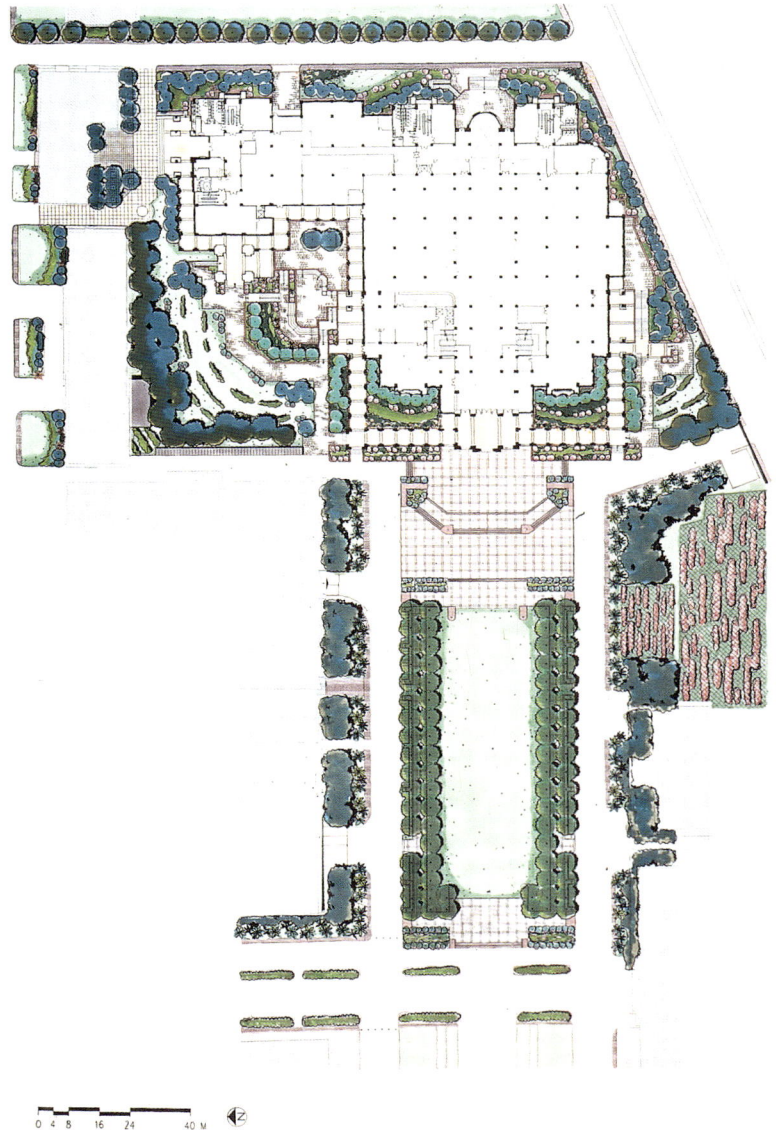

1

1 Ground floor plan
2 View from the southwest
3 Bell tower
4 View from the central boulevard

2

3

4

5 West elevation
6 View from the northwest
7 Sunken courtyard

5

0   12m

6

8 East side entrance
9 Open courtyard
10 View from the northeast
11 Reading space

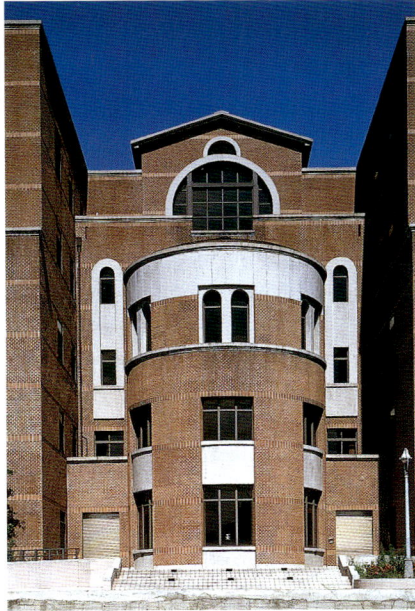
8

9

10

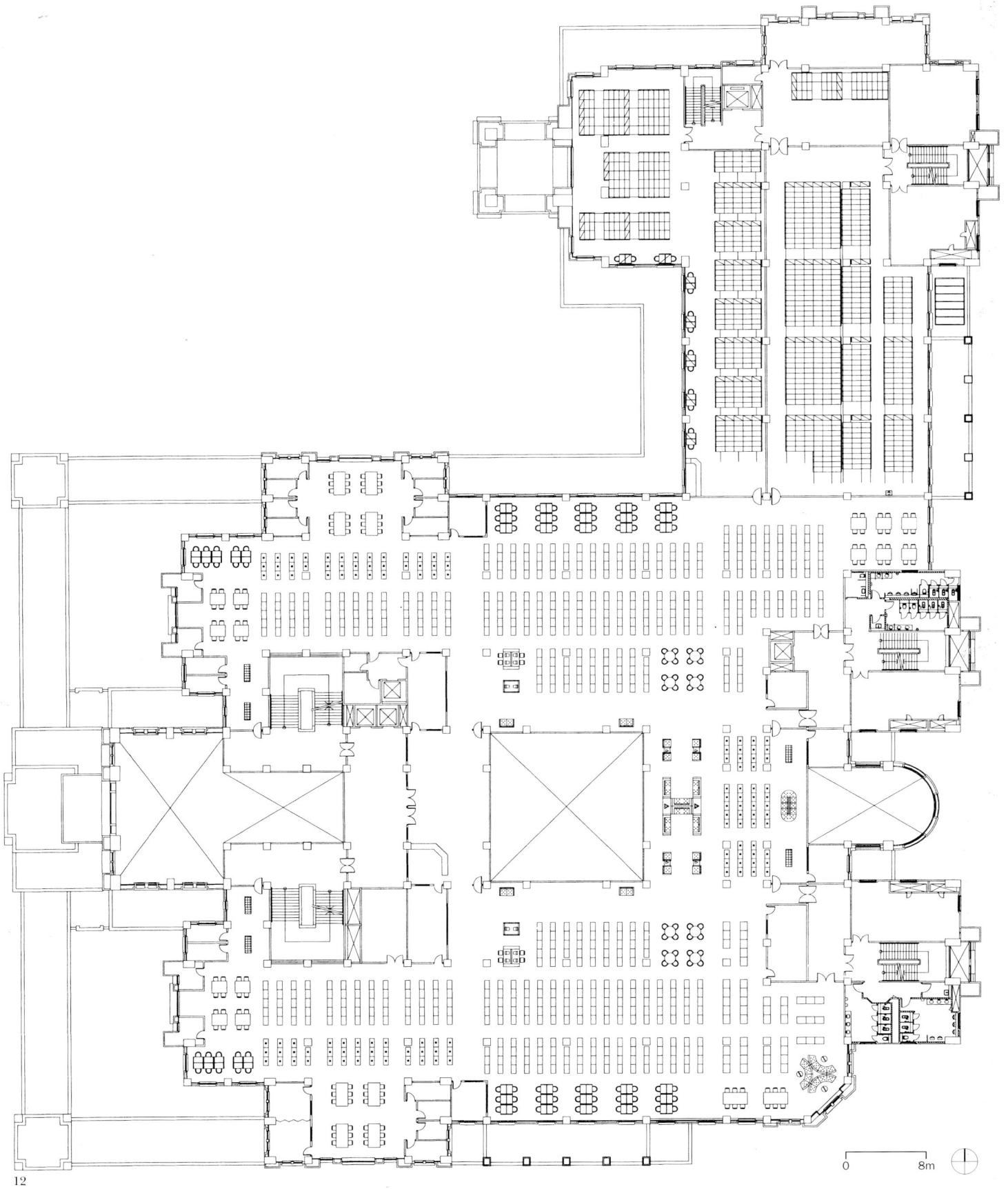

12 Second floor plan
13 Main lobby

12

13

15

14

14   Arcade
15–18 Reading space
19   Display hall

16

17

18

19

Sports Center, National Taiwan University

Design/Completion 1994/2001
Taipei, Taiwan
National Taiwan University
41,815.52 square meters
Membrane roof with steel structure and reinforced concrete

This new athletics and convocation complex for National Taiwan University was planned to blend in and support the campus development while, at the same time, providing a new, active image for the university. The large multi-function arena is both highly efficient and filled with natural light, while the many other activity spaces expand students' after-class life. The primary components of the program for this project include below-grade spaces for various sports, multi-function ball courts on the first level, and administrative and educational spaces on the second level, topped by the main arena, which seats up to 4,500 spectators.

This sports center design distinguishes itself by its responses to the specific characteristics of its site, defining one corner of the overall campus, facing the playing fields to the south, and with an elevated highway to the north. The design develops a complex and detailed response to the traditional materials and feeling of the campus, while at the same time relating to the elevated highway and providing a roof structure which will glow like a lantern at night, making an addition to Taipei's urban nightscape. Thus, in addition to providing the functional requirements of a modern campus sports complex, this project forms a link between the campus and its urban environment.

1

2

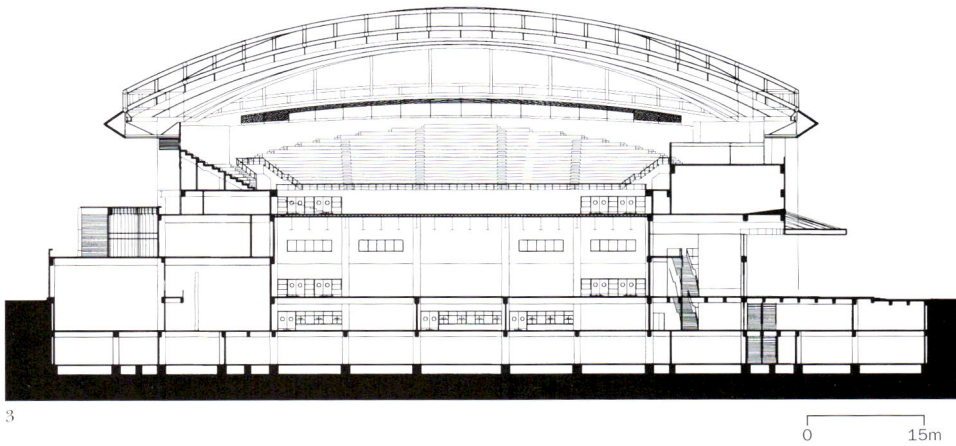

3

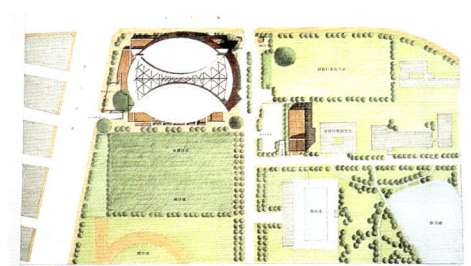

4

1   Aerial view from the east
2   View from the northeast
3   Longitudinal section
4   Site plan
5   View from the east

0   15m

5

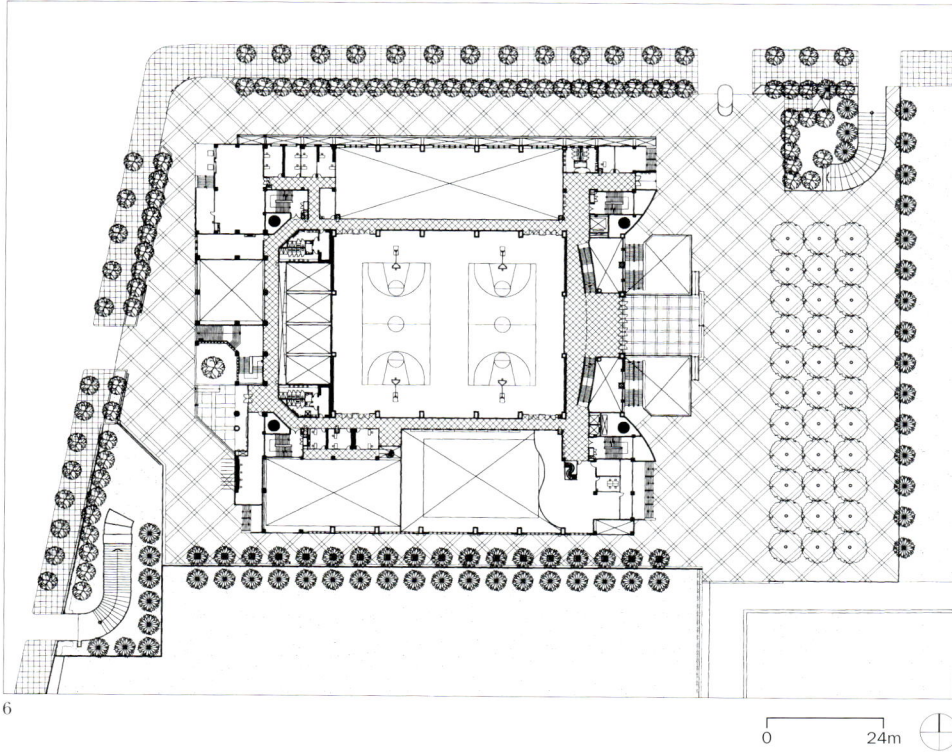

6

0　　　　24m

7

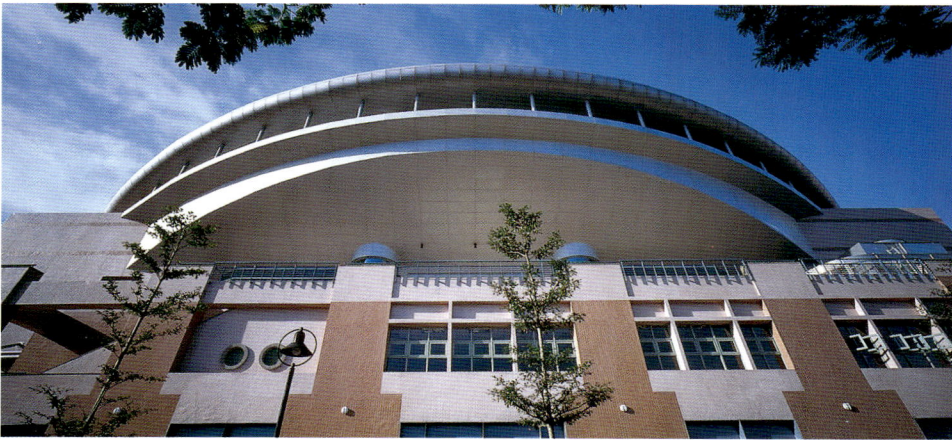

8

9

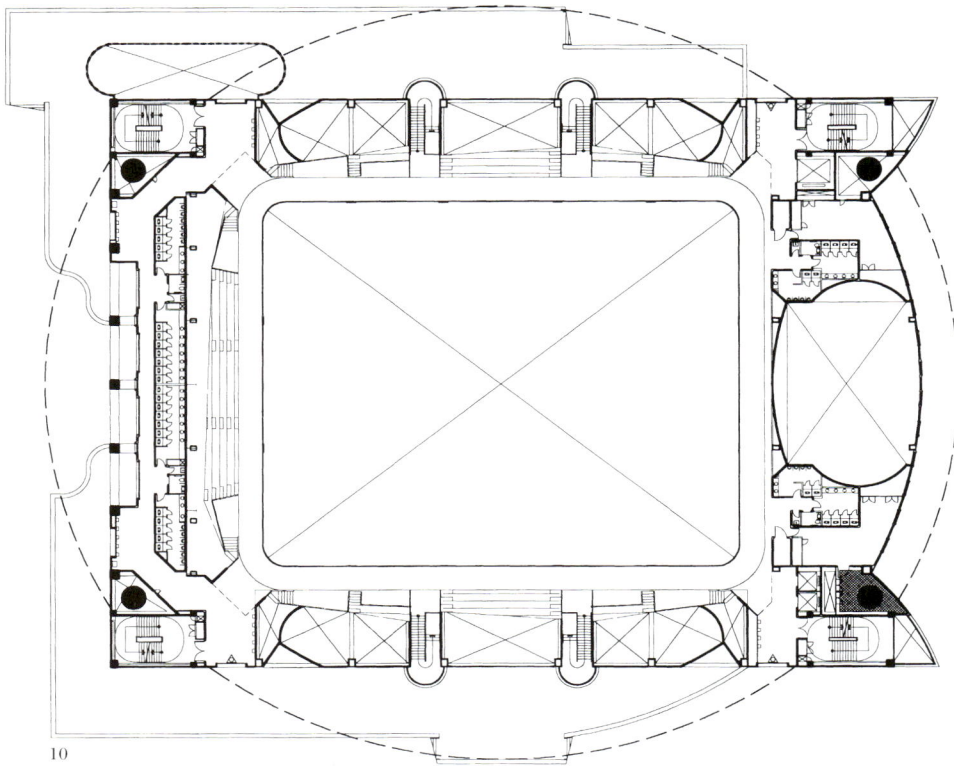

10

11

12

0   12m

Classroom Building, National Chung-Cheng University

Design/Completion 1989/1991
Chiayi, Taiwan
National Chung-Cheng University
13,168 square meters
Reinforced concrete
Red brick tile

The classroom building is located north of the campus's main east–west axis. The building entrance opens south, which directly faces the administration building across the main axis. It fulfills its purpose: to accentuate the main axis by having symmetrical wings which also reflect the uniqueness of the site.

The central garden provides students and teachers with a place of exchange and gathering. The experience of entering the building is heightened through multiple changes in space and scale. The majority of classrooms are placed on the northern and southern side of the building to achieve ultimate lighting conditions. The massive building elevation is visually broken up into smaller sections, but the coherence of the building is retained through its walls and roof. Red brick was chosen as the building's exterior wall finish to provide a friendly feeling to its occupants.

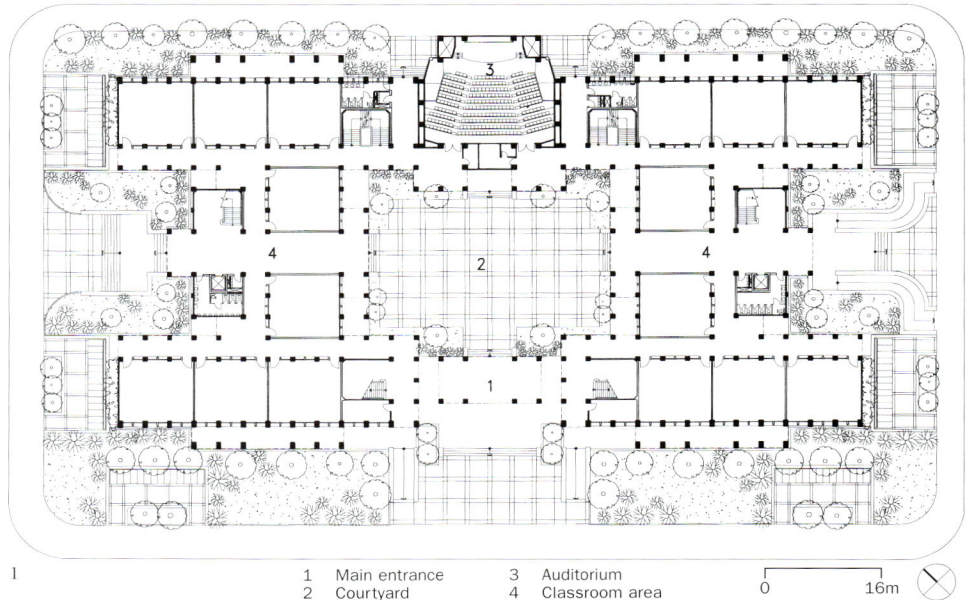

1

| 1 | Main entrance | 3 | Auditorium |
| 2 | Courtyard | 4 | Classroom area |

0   16m

2

1 First floor plan
2 View from the south
3 Main façade
4 View into courtyard
Following pages:
    Front façade

3

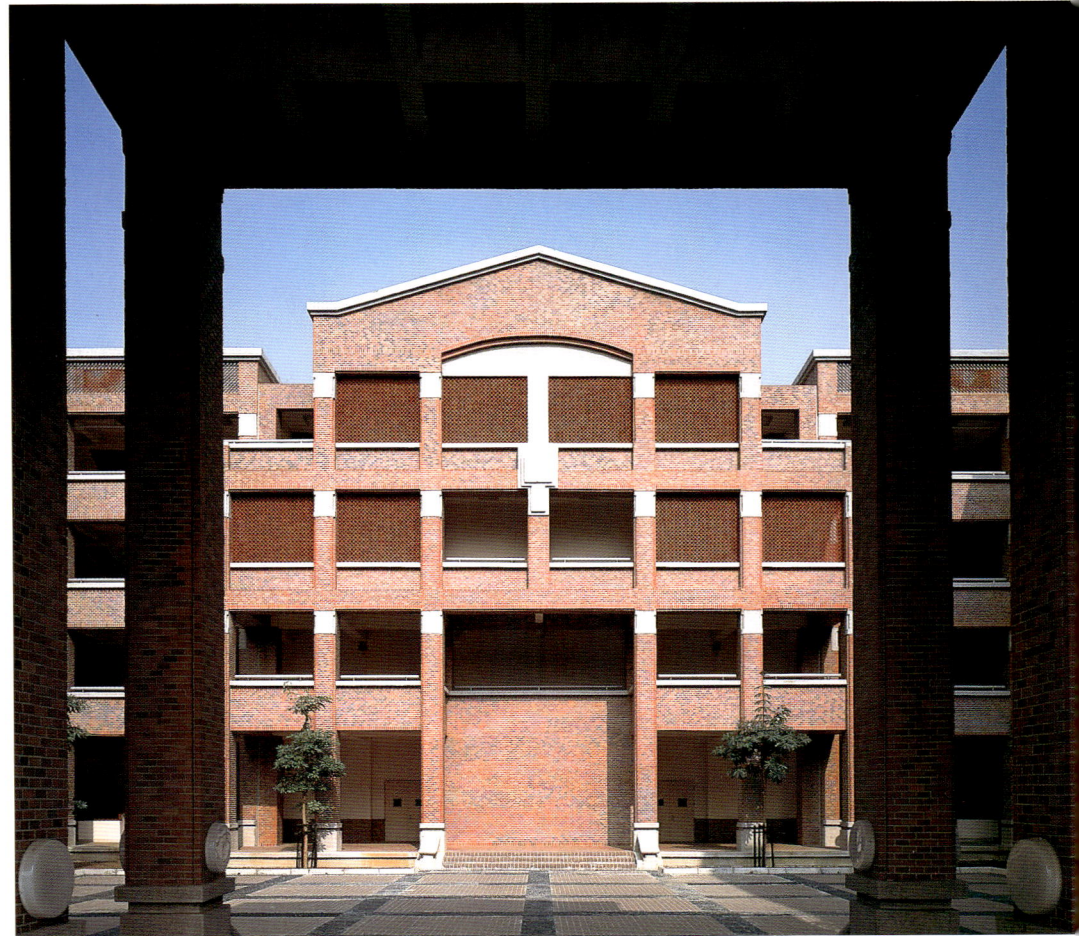

4

6 Section
7 View to main entrance porch
8 View from the east
9&10 Balcony of upper floor

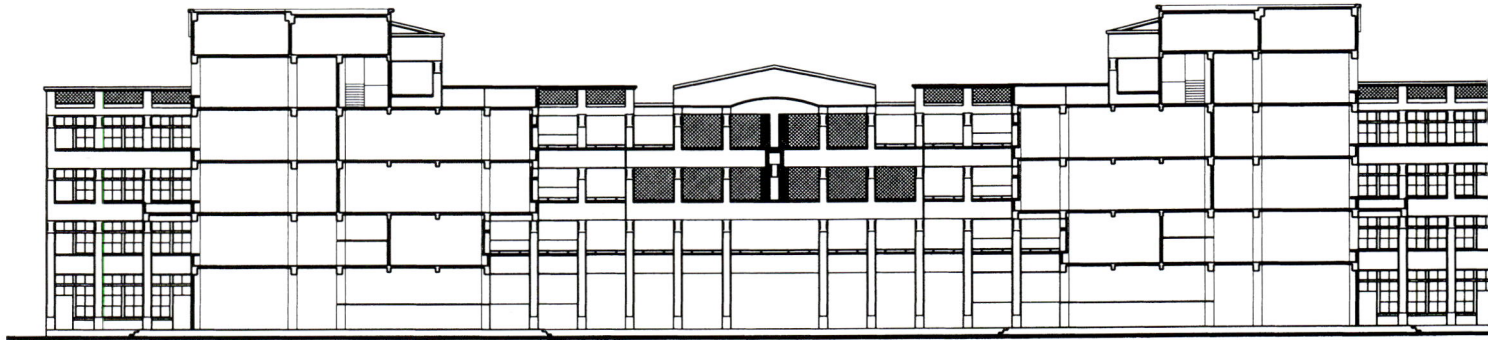

6

0

7

8

9

10

National Chung-Cheng University Assembly Hall

Design/Completion 1990/1994
Chiayi, Taiwan
National Chung-Cheng University
16,813 square meters
Steel structure

The Assembly Hall is located at the east end of the campus's east–west axis, and therefore is an axial focal point and of visual importance.

The Assembly Hall has a symmetrical design. With the site slightly raised, the main entrance aligns with the main axis and is linked by a set of grand stairs to provide students with a place for short gathering. Once up the stairs, the arcade extends to both wings to provide a semi-outdoor place. Meanwhile, it gives rhythm to the building's elevation and provides a friendlier scale to its occupants. The layering of walls at the center of the building not only gives the building a stable and solemn feel, but also serves as a visual focus. Red brick was chosen as the material for the exterior wall finish, to continue the existing coherence amongst the buildings on campus.

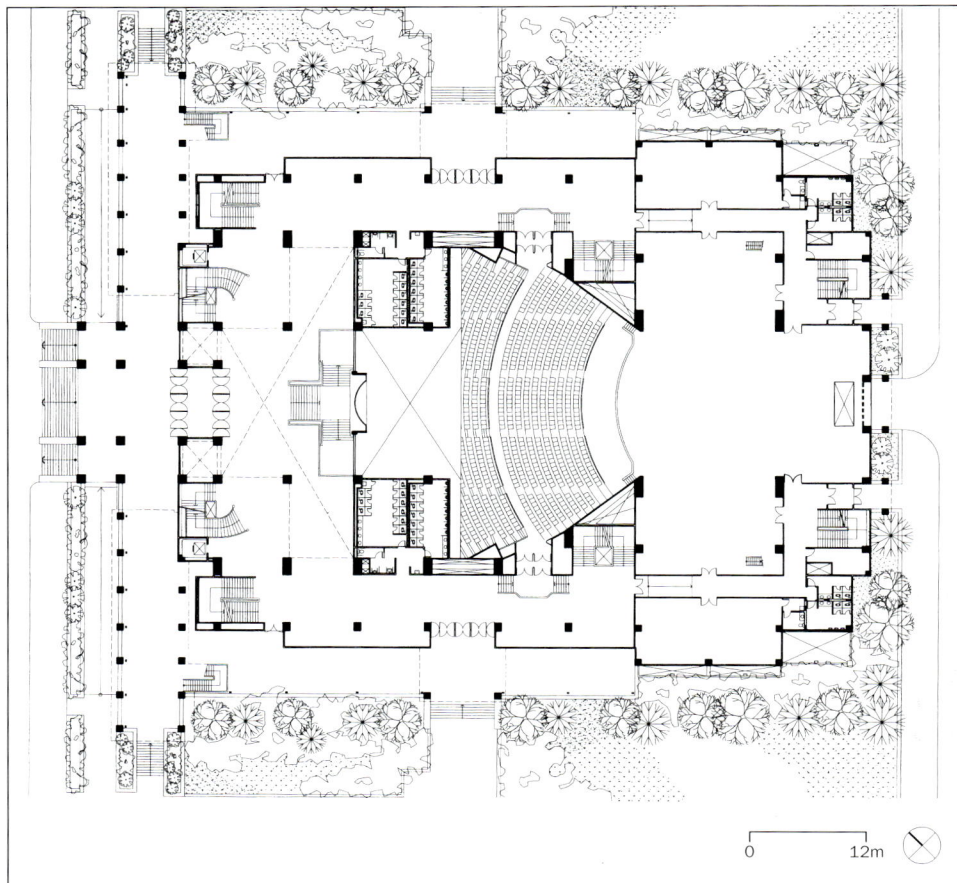

1

0　　　　　12m

1　First floor plan
2　View from the west
3　View from the south

2

4 Longitudinal section
5 Front façade
6 Auditorium

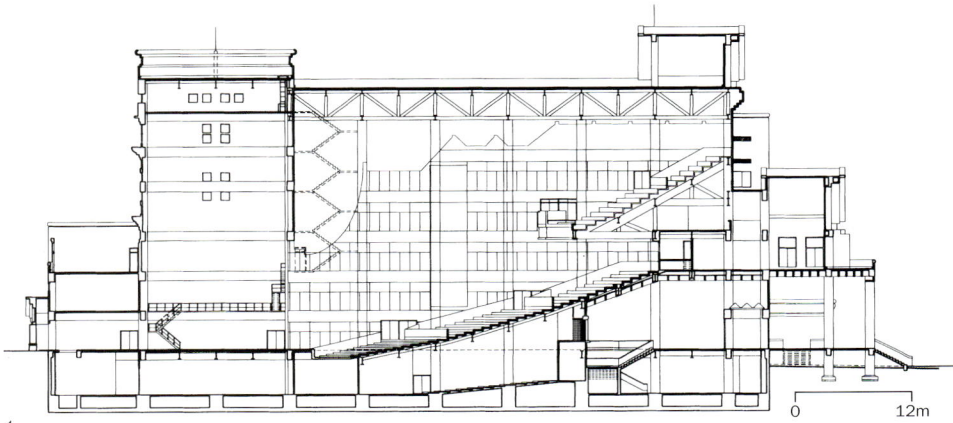

4

0   12m

5

6

College of Business, National Cheng-Chih University

Design/Completion 1993/1997
Taipei, Taiwan
National Cheng-Chih University
28,197.23 square meters
Reinforced concrete

Located beside the main entrance to National Cheng-Chih University in the Mucha suburb of Taipei, this 12-story building provides a landmark at the junction between academia and the commercial world.

The building is designed to relate to the modern buildings of the library and administration buildings, as well as to provide a student activity plaza which offers space from the adjacent original area of the campus. On the first floor there is an international conference facility, while the upper floors provide classrooms, professors' offices, the library, administrative offices, and a computerized teaching facility—all planned to provide for future development of the College.

Along with the client and contractor for this project, the firm was awarded the 1996 Award for Excellence in Construction Quality by the Executive Yuan. This award not only recognizes architects' responsibility for construction documents and supervision, but also highlights the successful partnership between the three parties responsible for the project.

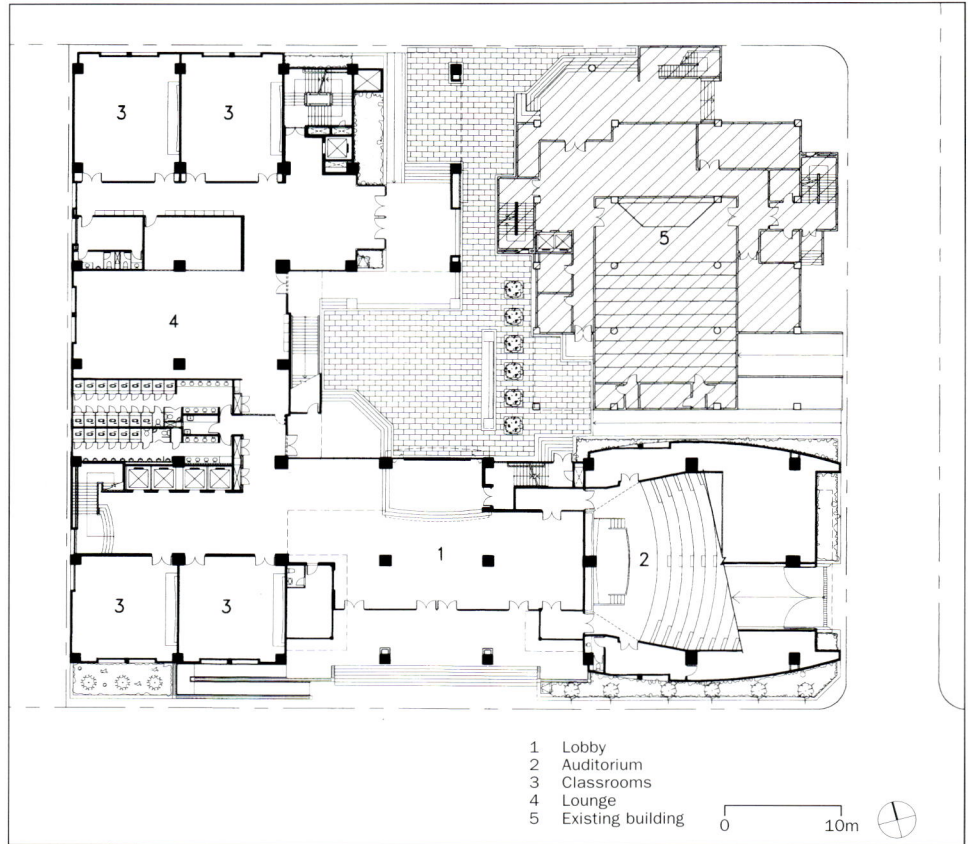

1 Lobby
2 Auditorium
3 Classrooms
4 Lounge
5 Existing building

0   10m

2

1

3

1   West elevation
2   First floor plan
3   Front façade
4   View from the southwest

4

5

Taipei American School
Campus Planning, Gymnasium,
and Academic Buildings

Design/Completion 1987/1989 (Phase I); 1988/1991 (Phase II)
Taipei, Taiwan
Taipei American School
46,220.57 square meters
Tile with steel reinforced concrete and steel structure

For the Taipei American School's new campus, located in the Tienmu district outside of Taipei, we were responsible for both the overall campus planning, which allowed for phased construction of the facility, as well as architectural design for all of the various buildings.

Providing a comprehensive educational program for 2,300 students from kindergarten through senior high school, the Taipei American School aimed to develop a model educational facility in Taipei. Under our planning and design, the campus includes classrooms, administration offices, music classrooms, cafeteria, library, auditorium, gymnasium, and indoor swimming pool. We were also responsible for the landscape design, including sports facilities (baseball field, a 400-meter track, tennis, and pelota courts), outdoor spaces for study or student performances, as well as parking.

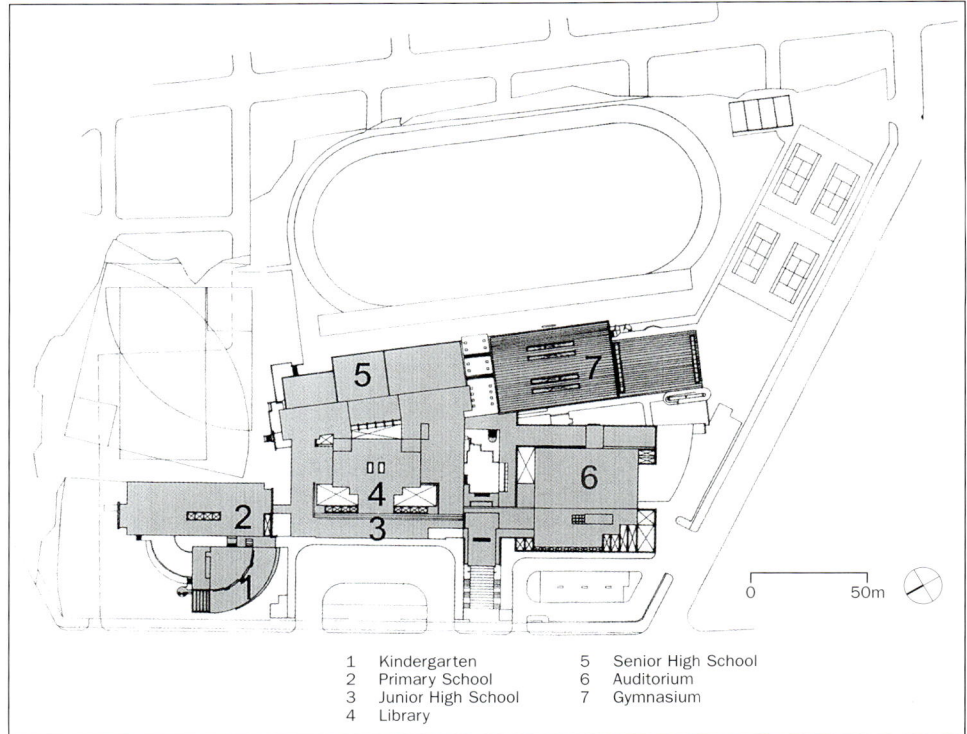

1	Kindergarten	5	Senior High School
2	Primary School	6	Auditorium
3	Junior High School	7	Gymnasium
4	Library		

1

2

1 Site plan
2 Entry plaza looking toward north
3 Main entrance
4 Classroom building at the north
5 Open space of the campus

3

4

5

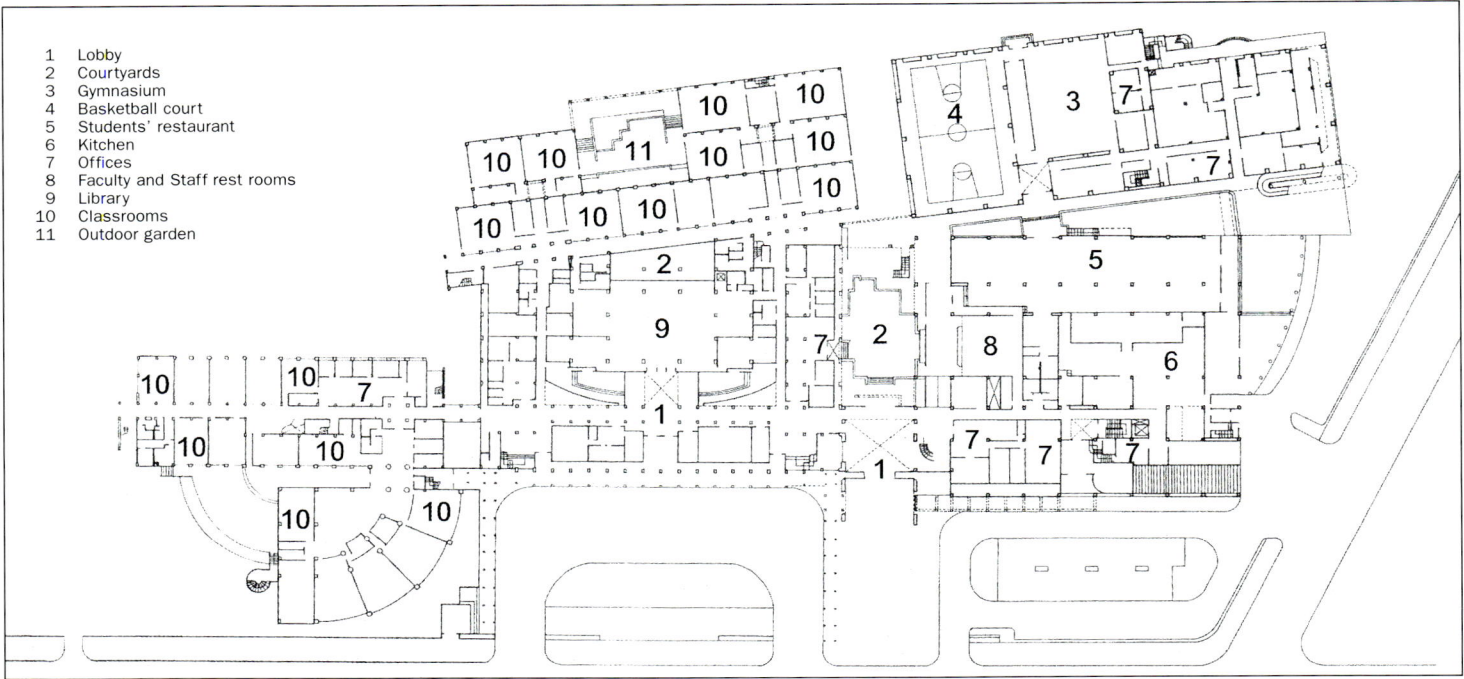

1 Lobby
2 Courtyards
3 Gymnasium
4 Basketball court
5 Students' restaurant
6 Kitchen
7 Offices
8 Faculty and Staff rest rooms
9 Library
10 Classrooms
11 Outdoor garden

6

8

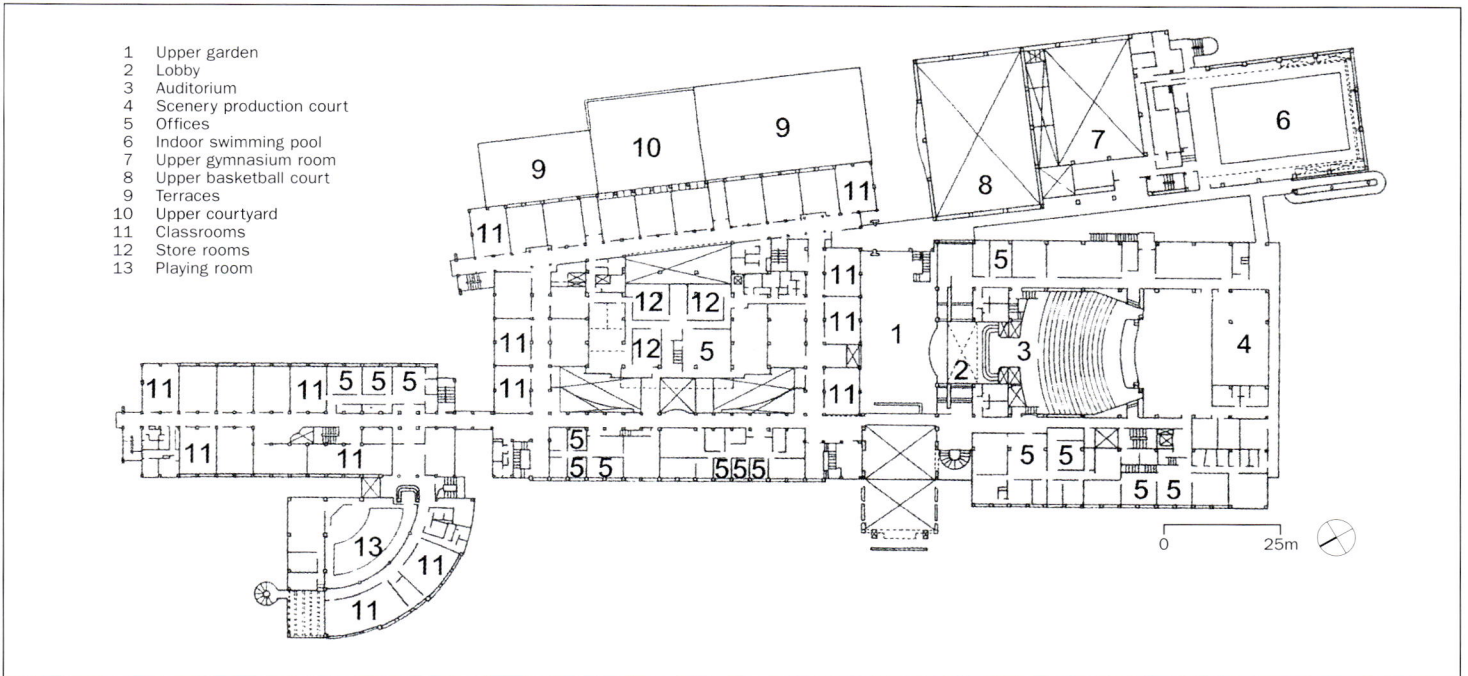

1 Upper garden
2 Lobby
3 Auditorium
4 Scenery production court
5 Offices
6 Indoor swimming pool
7 Upper gymnasium room
8 Upper basketball court
9 Terraces
10 Upper courtyard
11 Classrooms
12 Store rooms
13 Playing room

7

9   Main entrance looking toward south
11 Entry plaza
10 Main lobby
12 Auditorium

10

11

12

Library and Information Center, National Kaohsiung First University of Science and Technology

Design/Completion 1997/2001
Kaohsiung, Taiwan
National Kaohsiung First University of Science and Technology
26,430 square meters
Reinforced concrete

This building includes the library, computer center, audio-visual center, international conference hall, and self-learning center. The site is located at the heart of the school campus and is an important connection point between east and west campuses.

The objective of this design is not only to respect and strengthen the spatial structure of the campus, but more importantly, to refute the fallacy that a building can only have a single aspect. The library is designed to be accessible from all directions. Students and faculty from all over the campus can wander through the building.

Aside from the necessary service space, the spatial organization adapts an open and flexible layout. Under this layout, there is an inner court facing the campus which links each of the floors. The sky-lit window on top of the inner court brings in the sunlight, creating bright and rich changes to the rooms.

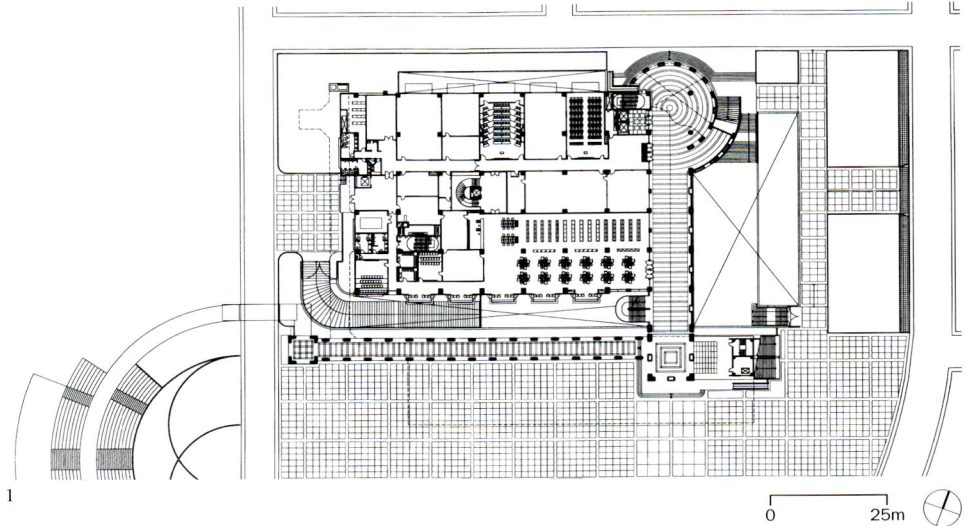

1

0   25m

2

48

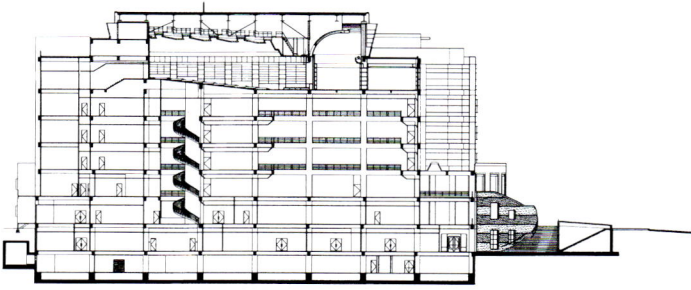
3

4

5

6

7

9

8

10

Library and Information Center, National Chiayi University

Design/Completion 2000/2004
Chiayi, Taiwan
National Chiayi University
23,254 square meters
Deep-set windows with reinforced concrete

The library is located at the geometrical center of the campus. In its location alongside the Mathematics building and the Engineering building, this area becomes the new focus for the campus with a central space. It provides the campus with a new spatial order. In order to satisfy the demands for various services and to establish a campus-wide digitizing information system for the future, flexibility of space has been the design principle in the layout.

The design aims to create an elegant and composed structure as the focal point of the campus. Since the school is located in an area of strong seismic activity, its structural design needs to be symmetrical and square in shape. The façade of the building is designed with sunshades to provide protection from exposure to the east–west path of the sun.

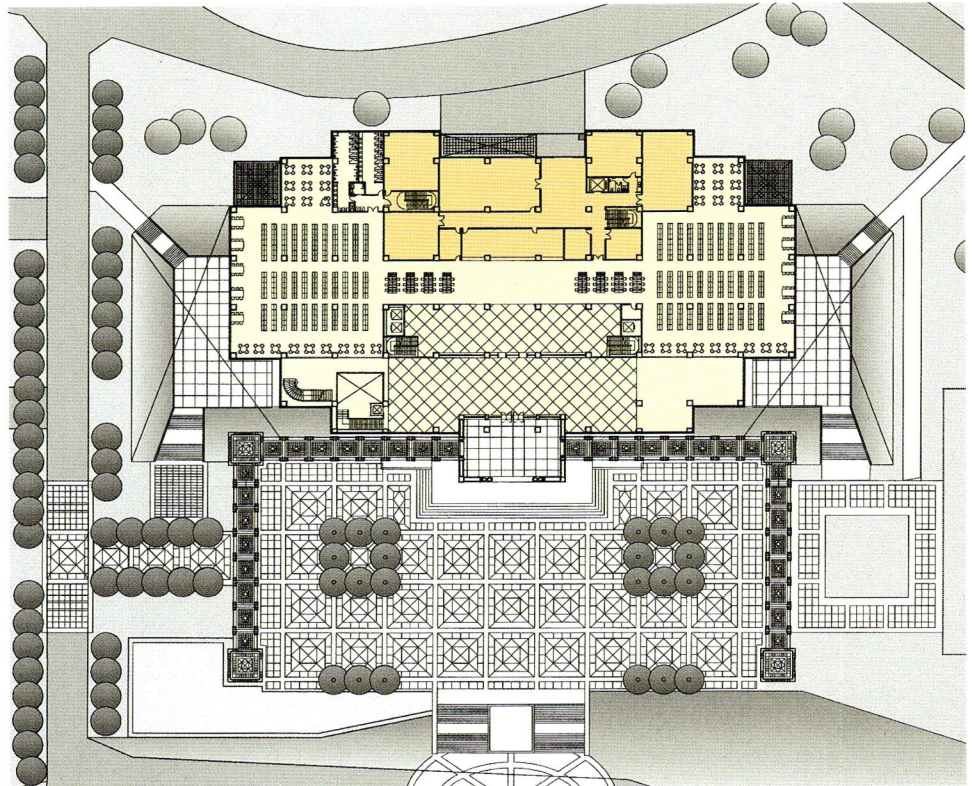

2

0   18m

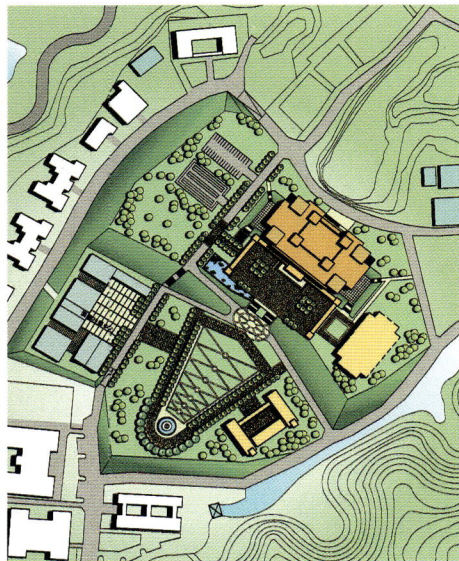

1

3

1 Site plan
2 First floor plan
3 Front elevation
4 Rendering of aerial view
5 East elevation
6 View from the west

Public/Government

Exhibition Center, Taipei World Trade Center

Design/Completion 1981/1985
Taipei, Taiwan
Ministry of Economic Affairs, Executive Yuan
157,705 square meters
Reinforced concrete
Tile and granite exterior
Joint-venture firm: HOK, USA

This project is the keystone in the master plan for the overall Taipei World Trade Center. It contains various facilities that provide for international trade shows and exhibitions, including a hall for temporary exhibits, spaces for long-term trade exhibits, and support businesses for exhibition visitors. The massing of the building is designed to break down the large scale of this building, integrating it into the adjacent Hsinyi redevelopment area.

The building provides direct connections to both the Grand Hyatt Hotel and the World Trade Center Office Building, with access to public transportation, enclosed parking, and to a large public plaza. The interior spaces are arranged around a spacious central atrium, which is enlivened by visitors moving from floor to floor via escalators through the exhibitions.

Preliminary design and design development of this portion of the World Trade Center complex were by the American architectural consultant, HOK. This project is an example of incorporating international standards and expertise in a Taiwan project, providing for both foreign businesses and local needs. As such, the project has become an important part of the international business world of Taiwan, and also of the life of Taipei residents.

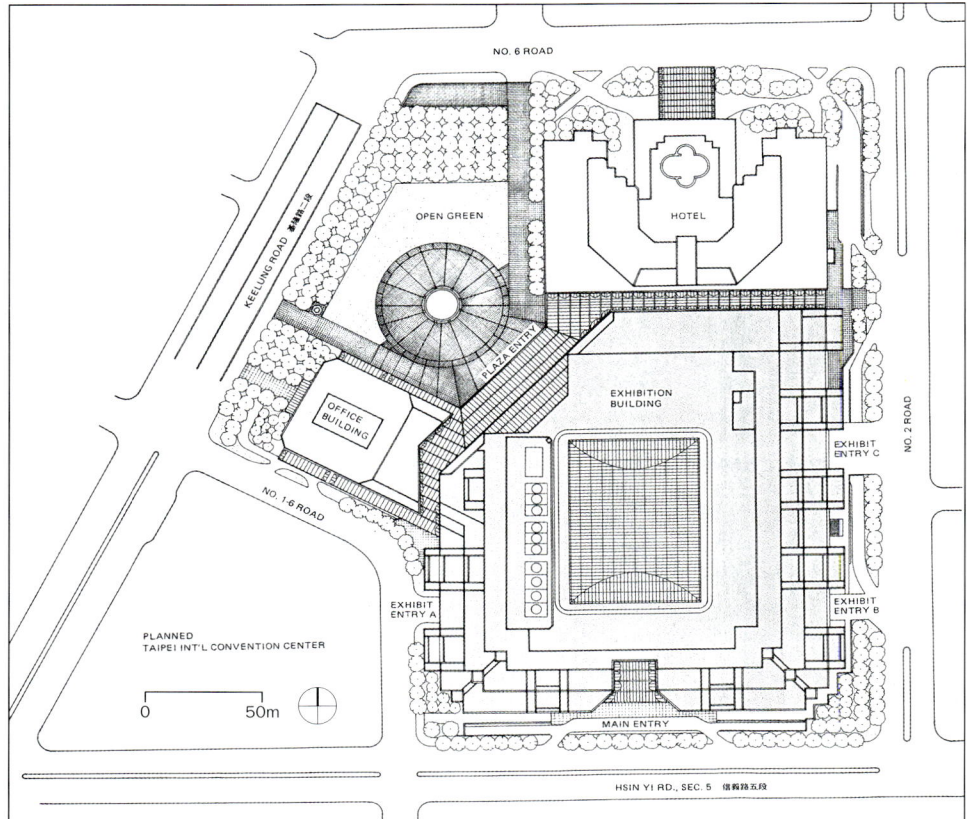

1

2

1 Site plan
2 View from the southeast
3 Side elevation
4 Main entrance

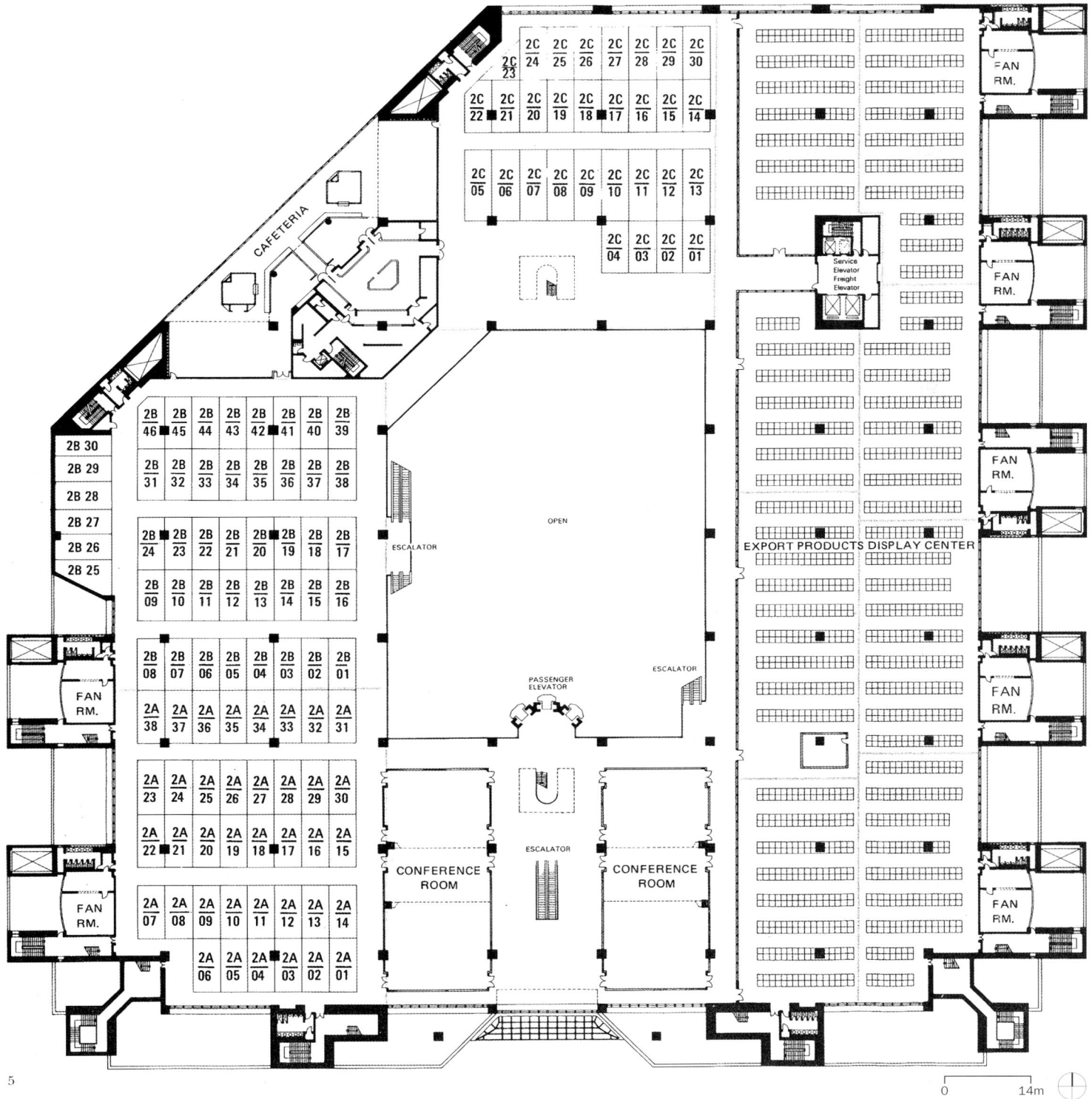

2C/23	2C/24	2C/25	2C/26	2C/27	2C/28	2C/29	2C/30
2C/22	2C/21	2C/20	2C/19	2C/18	2C/17	2C/16	2C/15	2C/14
2C/05	2C/06	2C/07	2C/08	2C/09	2C/10	2C/11	2C/12	2C/13
2C/04	2C/03	2C/02	2C/01

CAFETERIA

Service Elevator
Freight Elevator

FAN RM.

EXPORT PRODUCTS DISPLAY CENTER

2B 30
2B 29
2B 28
2B 27
2B 26
2B 25

2B/46	2B/45	2B/44	2B/43	2B/42	2B/41	2B/40	2B/39
2B/31	2B/32	2B/33	2B/34	2B/35	2B/36	2B/37	2B/38
2B/24	2B/23	2B/22	2B/21	2B/20	2B/19	2B/18	2B/17
2B/09	2B/10	2B/11	2B/12	2B/13	2B/14	2B/15	2B/16
2B/08	2B/07	2B/06	2B/05	2B/04	2B/03	2B/02	2B/01
2A/38	2A/37	2A/36	2A/35	2A/34	2A/33	2A/32	2A/31
2A/23	2A/24	2A/25	2A/26	2A/27	2A/28	2A/29	2A/30
2A/22	2A/21	2A/20	2A/19	2A/18	2A/17	2A/16	2A/15
2A/07	2A/08	2A/09	2A/10	2A/11	2A/12	2A/13	2A/14
2A/06	2A/05	2A/04	2A/03	2A/02	2A/01

OPEN

ESCALATOR

ESCALATOR

PASSENGER ELEVATOR

ESCALATOR

FAN RM.

CONFERENCE ROOM

CONFERENCE ROOM

FAN RM.

FAN RM.

FAN RM.

5

0   14m

5

Convention Center, Taipei World Trade Center

Design/Completion 1984/1989
Taipei, Taiwan
Ministry of Economic Affairs, Executive Yuan
60,000 square meters
Steel structure
Tile and granite exterior

The functions of this facility were planned to supplement each of the adjacent portions of the Taipei World Trade Center complex, including the exhibition center, office building, and hotel. The building design, with its stepped-back forms and selection of exterior materials, harmonizes with the design of these facilities, while the site plan provides a public park and fountain, marking a major intersection in the city.

The interior contains a flexible combination of facilities and spaces for both international and domestic meetings of various sizes. The spaces range from the large 3,500-seat auditorium, to smaller auditoriums (both fixed-seat and convertible), function spaces and meeting rooms. Overall, the goal of this project was to provide the optimum in flexibility and technical support for the rapidly changing requirements of a broad variety of different meeting types. In addition, the logistics of providing separate service and public circulation were effectively resolved for this constricted site.

1 View from the southeast
2 Front elevation

1

2

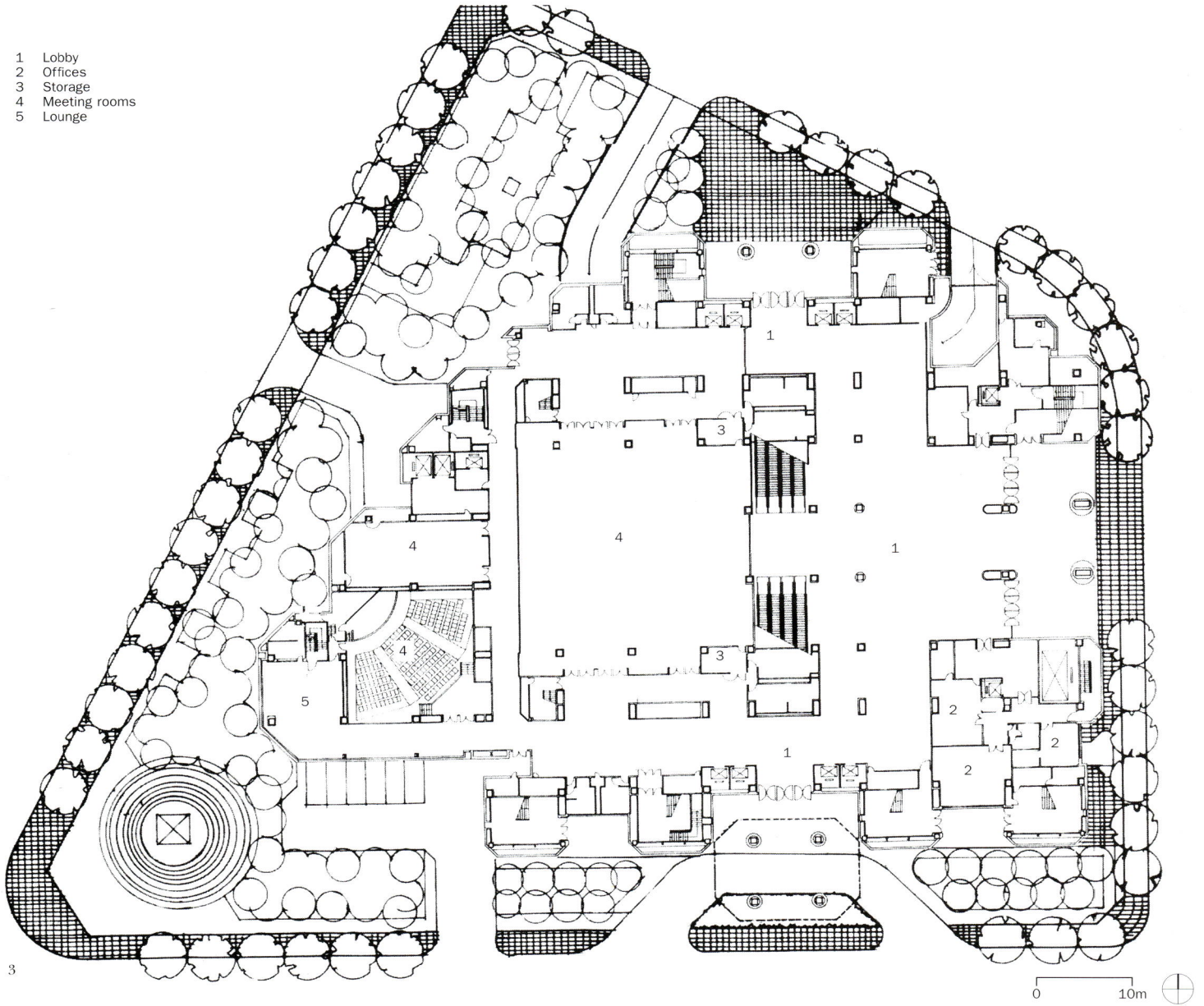

1   Lobby
2   Offices
3   Storage
4   Meeting rooms
5   Lounge

3

0   10m

3   First floor plan
4   Main lobby
5   Meeting room
6   International meeting room

4

7   Cross section
8   Plenary hall, view from stage
9   Plenary hall, view to stage

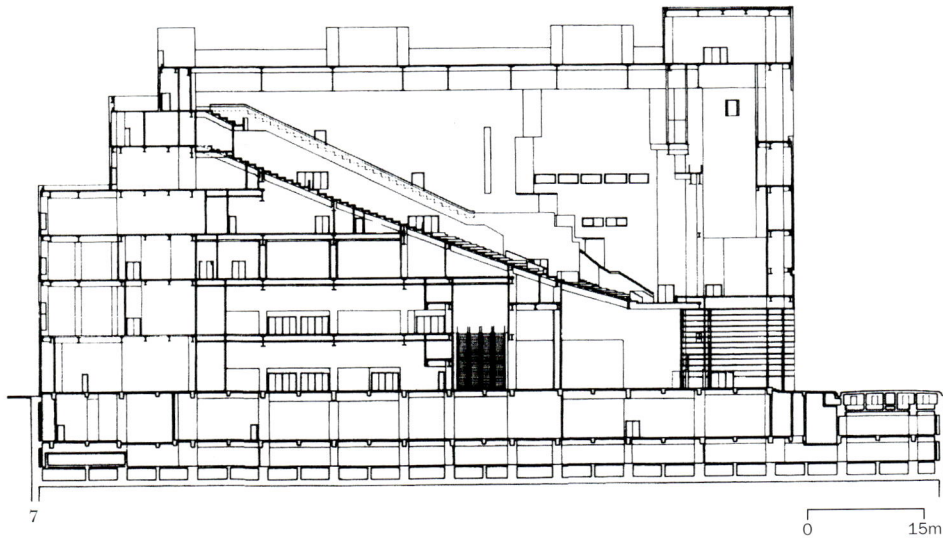

7

0   15m

8

9

Nantou County Municipal Office Building

Design/Completion 2000/2001
Nantou, Taiwan
Nantou County Government
46,606 square meters
Reinforced concrete
Tile exterior

The site is located on the south side of Nantou City. The concept behind this design is to provide a friendly environment that allows for leisure activities and encourages interaction between the people and the county.

Within the concept of "green architecture," the proposed design combines the natural environment and the local culture to form a distinctive architectural style. The design incorporates roof overhangs and shading devices to accentuate the effects of light and shadow. And, with the layering of green design, a new architectural style true to local culture and tradition is presented.

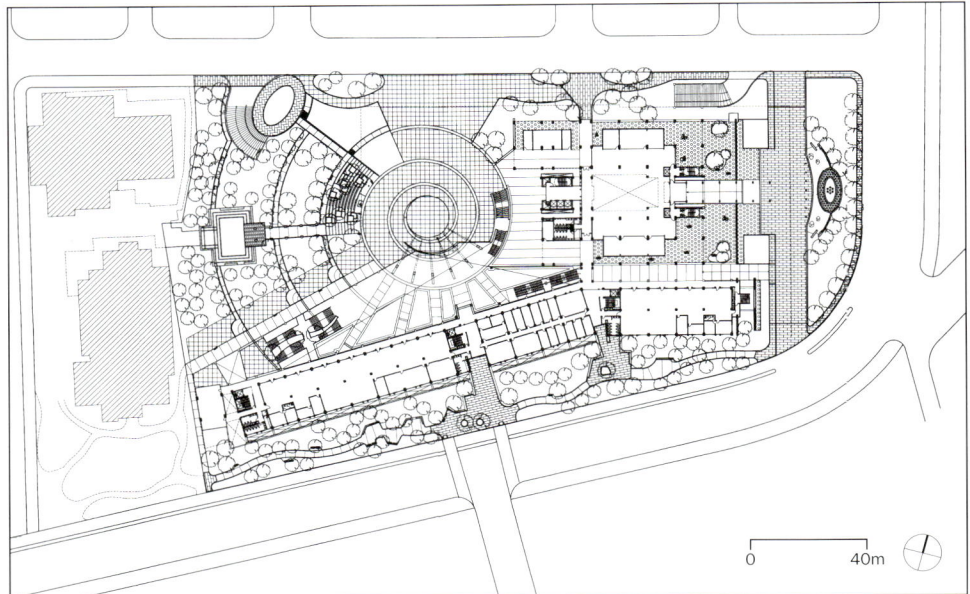

1

2

3

4

5

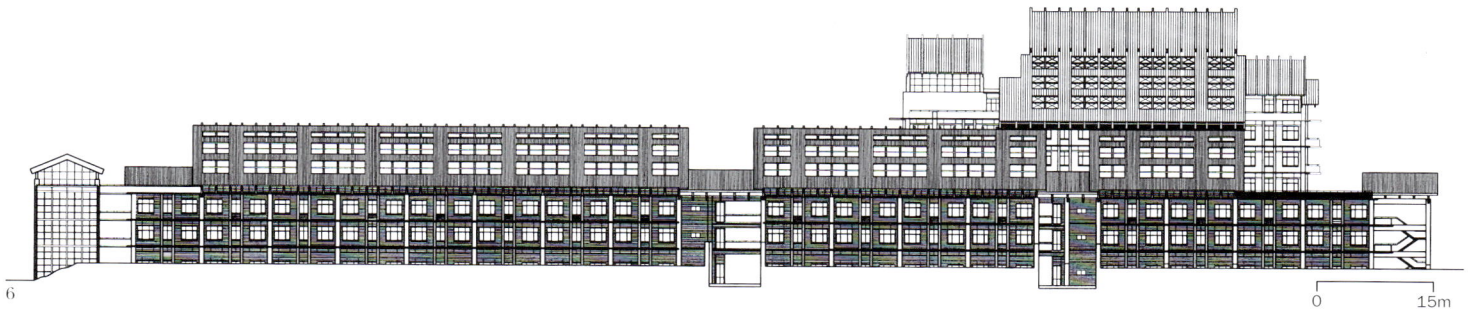

1 First floor plan
2&3 Study rendering for night view
4&5 Study rendering
6 South elevation
7 View from the southwest
8 View of the entry gallery
9 View from the northwest

The New Taichung City Civic Center

Design (Competition) 1995
Taichung, Taiwan
Taichung City Government
Reinforced concrete

The site of The New Taichung City Civic Center, including both the City Hall and the City Council Conference Hall, is located at the edge of Taichung city in a newly developed area. This site, once developed, will be the city's second focal point that is different from the old Taichung downtown. Currently, the site is empty, with only a few governmental facilities nearby.

The purpose of this project is to create a landmark building that the people of Taichung can be proud of. It is expected that the Civic Center will be a public and friendly place through which people can pass freely, and also serve as a symbol of democracy. The design of the City Hall has two wings opening to both sides and layers of recessed platforms to guide people into its open plaza. From there, the space is linked into the administration levels through the transition of different spaces. The City Hall, therefore, has a spatial quality that is inviting to the people and has a feeling of monumentality. In contrast with the dramatic and sculptural entity of the Council Conference Hall, the City Hall serves as a focal point in the City Civic Center. The Council Conference Hall, by comparison, has a more conservative and cleaner look.

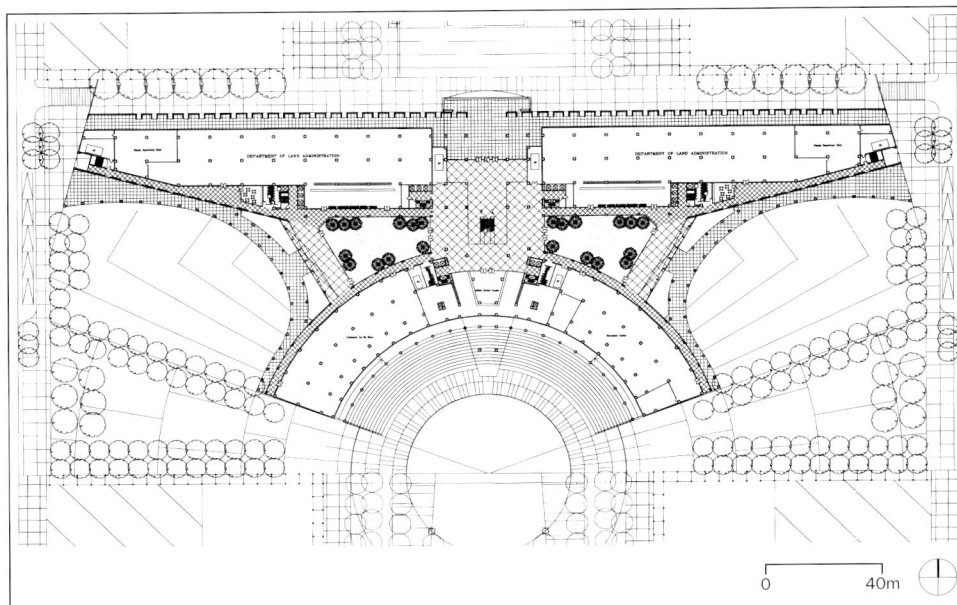

1

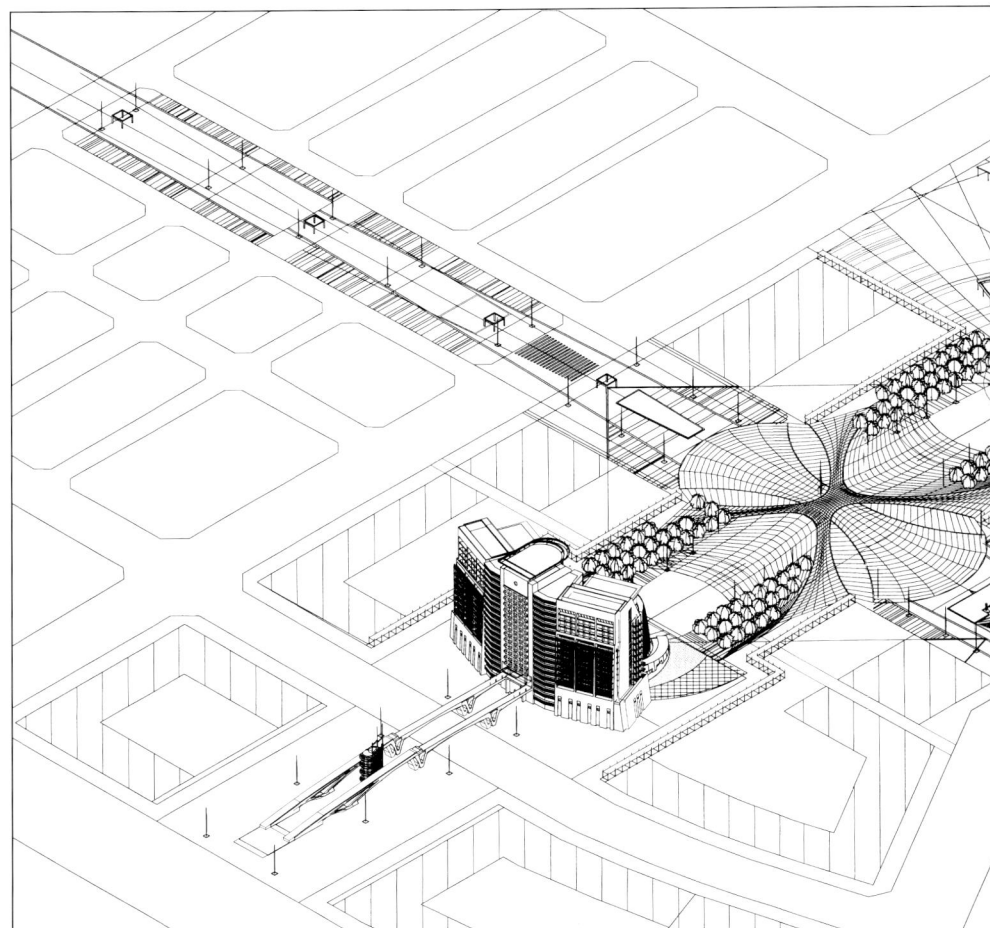

1   City government first floor plan
2   Axonometric of site plan
3   Longitudinal section
4   Front elevation of city government
5   Rendering of city council

2

3

0   60m

4

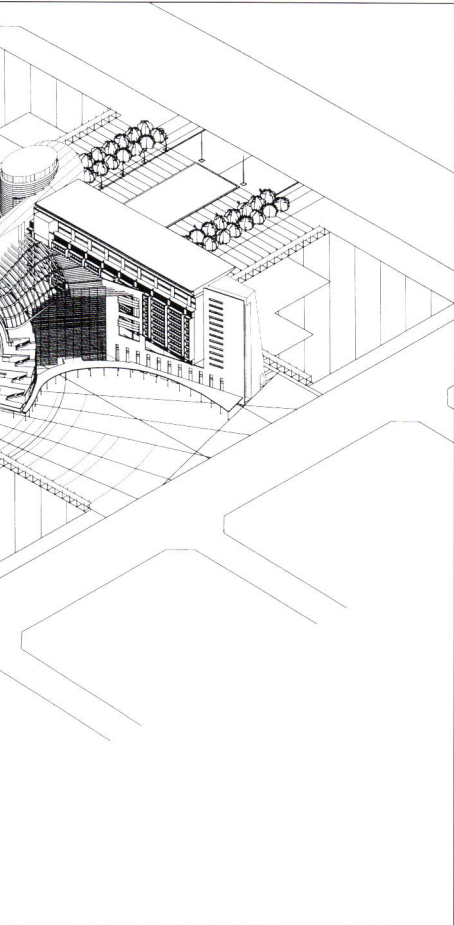

5

Kaohsiung Postal Processing Center

Competition 1995
Kaohsiung, Taiwan
General Post Office

This building is on a very difficult site among factory buildings; it faces the narrow opening of the freeway. The main feature this project uses is an arc-shaped wall to separate the administrative office area from the operating area. The office area is designed with a variety of different components of arc-shaped surfaces and hanging plates. Such a combination helps to blend this building into the environment of the gloomy and huge industrial factory buildings.

1

1   Perspective rendering
2   Cross section
3   Site plan
4   Cross section

2

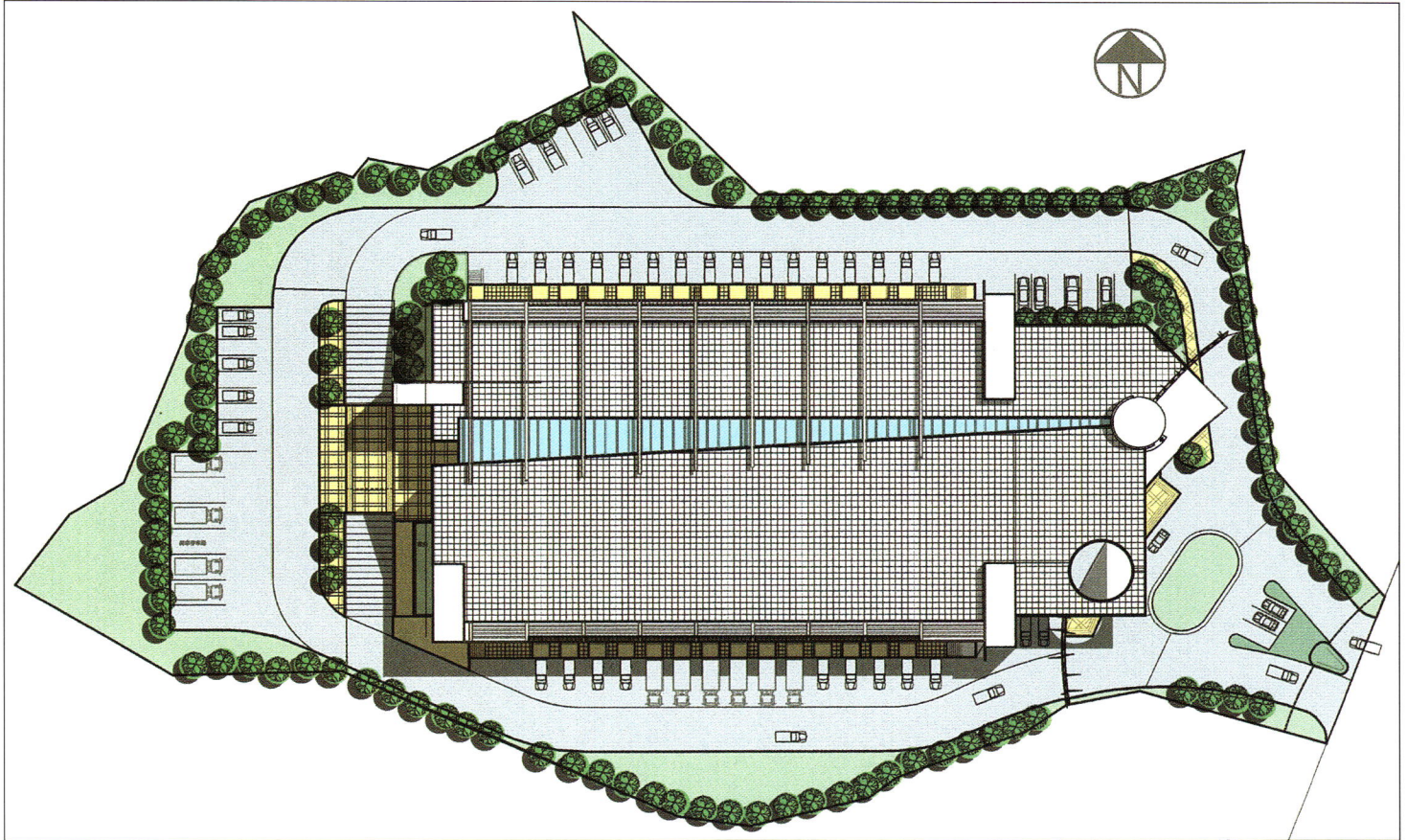

3

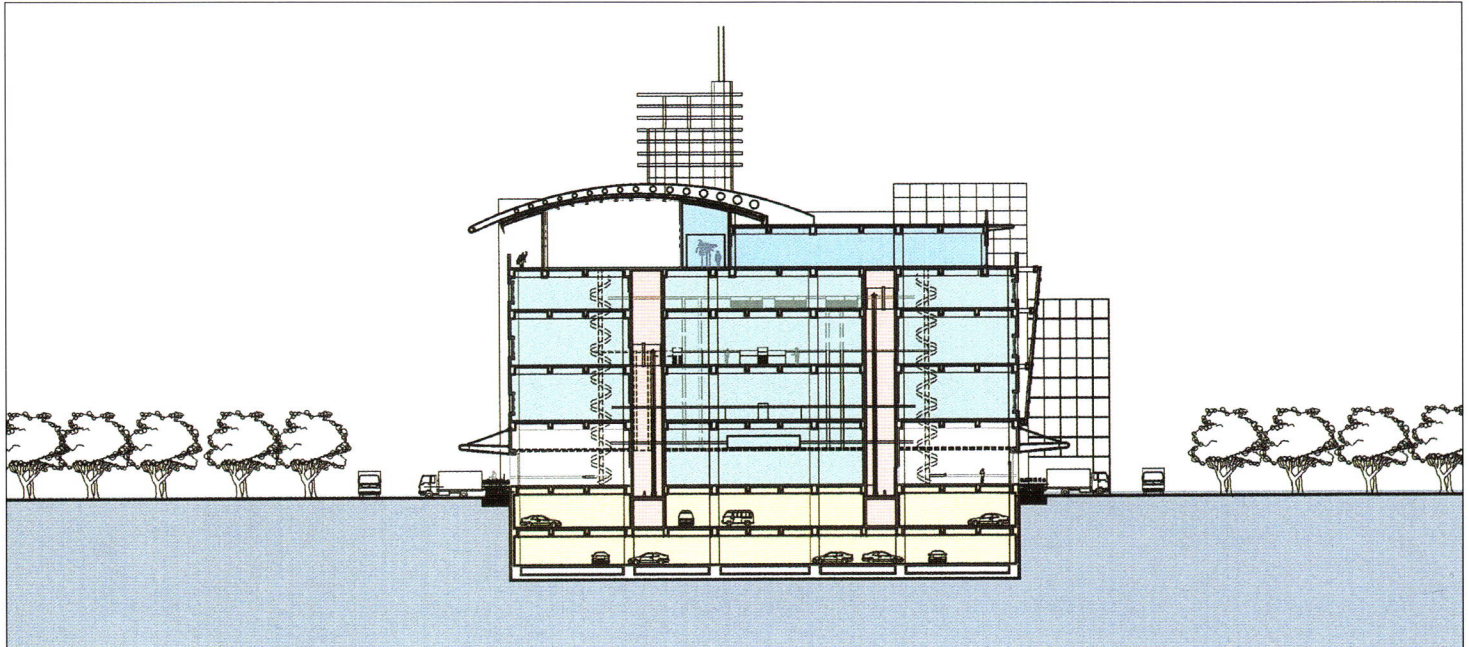

4

Commercial

Chia-Hsin Building

Design/Completion 1964/1967
Taipei, Taiwan
Chia-Hsin Cement Company
20,410 square meters
Steel reinforced concrete
Joint-venture architect: Eric Cumine, HK

Completed in 1967, the Chia-Hsin Building marks a milestone in Taiwan's high-rise office buildings. It is also the first office building in which a foreign architecture firm participated in the actual design. The firm designed this building with the architecture firm Eric Cumine of Hong Kong.

The solidity and neo-classic design of this building reflects the aesthetics views and expectations of a large office building at that time. The design is divided into three separate sections: crown, body, and base. The treatment of its fine portions, lines, and shadows were all carefully designed to capture a balanced unification.

In terms of its structural system, the building uses steel reinforced concrete. It was the first time this new system was introduced in Taiwan—a breakthrough in the local construction technology.

1

1 View from the northeast
2 First floor plan
3 Main entrance

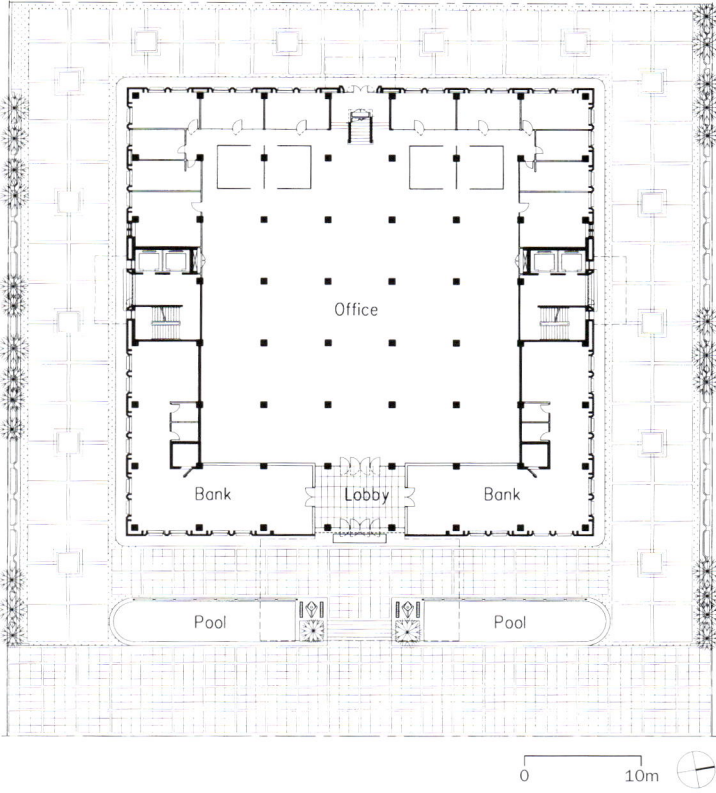

2

0   10m

3

Chung-Hsin Textile Company Headquarters

Design/Completion 1983/1986
Taipei, Taiwan
Chung-Hsin Textile Co. Ltd
24,387 square meters
Steel reinforced concrete
Gray aluminium curtainwall panels

This corporate headquarters for one of Taiwan's well-established corporations is located at a major intersection of Taipei's main commercial boulevard, Chunghsiao East Road. In this prominent location, the building is designed as a landmark which provides specific references to the trademarks of the corporation. The strong bi-axial symmetry of the building refers to the company name, Central Textile Corporation, while the tapered profile is reminiscent of its corporate logo. In addition, the rectangular window grid and pattern of joints in the curtainwall panels create a pattern similar to textiles, the company's main product.

The building's exterior is further distinguished by the use of light-gray aluminium curtainwall panels, which were an innovative material in Taiwan at the time of the building's construction. These panels, which are insulated to provide energy savings, also require relatively little maintenance to preserve their appearance. In addition, the matte surface of the panels are glare-free, making this building a good neighbor to its surroundings, as well as a distinctive corporate symbol.

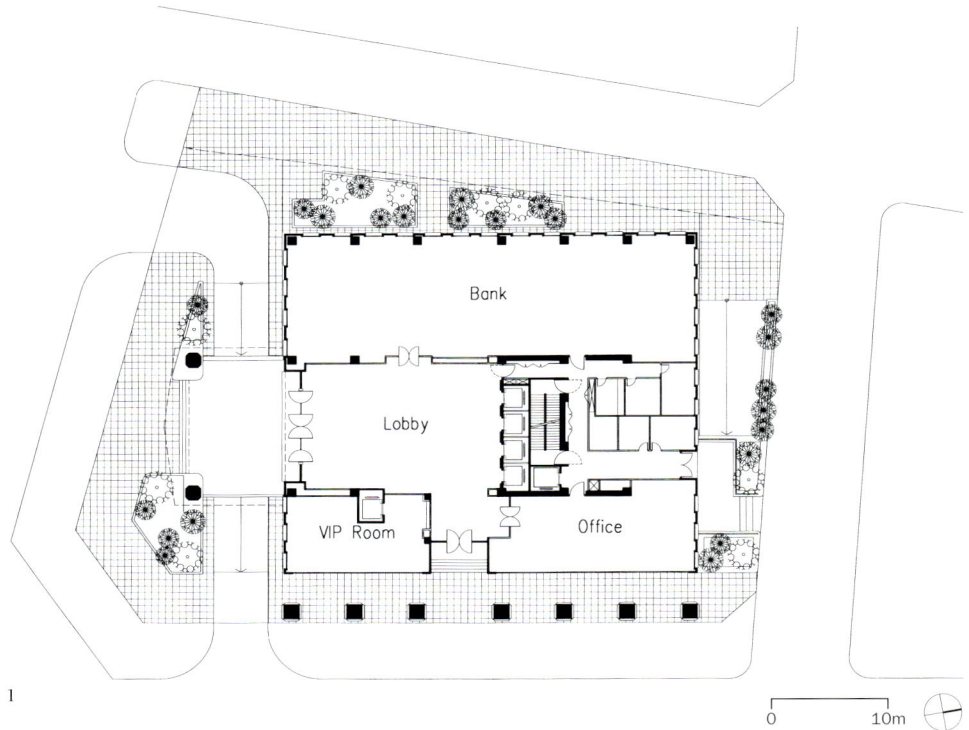

1

1   First floor plan
2   Partial view
3   Canopy skylight
Opposite:
    View from the northeast

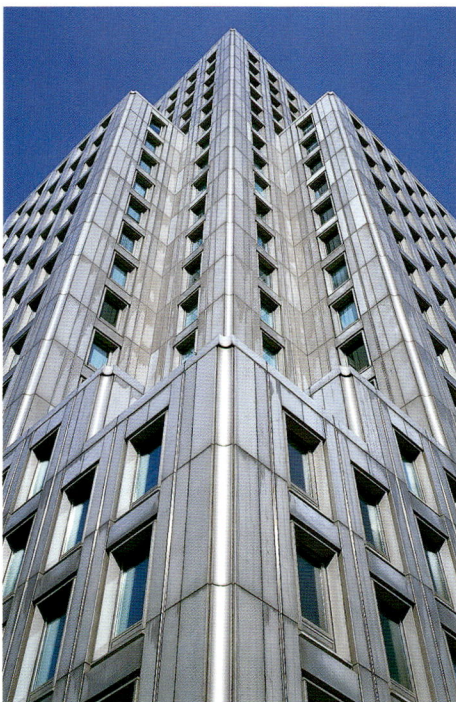

2

3

76

Grand Hyatt Hotel, Taipei

Design/Completion 1983/1989
Taipei, Taiwan
Hong-Leong Hotel Development Ltd
116,000 square meters
Reinforced concrete
Granite exterior

A member of the "Grand" class of Hyatt Hotels, the Taipei Hyatt Regency is a part of Taipei's most prestigious business development, the World Trade Convention Center and Offices. Since its construction in 1989, this hotel has helped to set the standard for luxury accommodation in the city.

The hotel's U-shaped plan provides the 860 guest rooms with dramatic views of the adjacent Sun Yat-Sen Memorial and the municipal government offices. These guest accommodations sit on top of a podium of hospitality and conference facilities.

A skylight for the main lobby provides an atrium for the entrance hall. An outdoor swimming pool and recreational facilities are also designed on the roof top of the podium.

1   Front plaza
2   Fifth floor plan
3   First floor plan

1

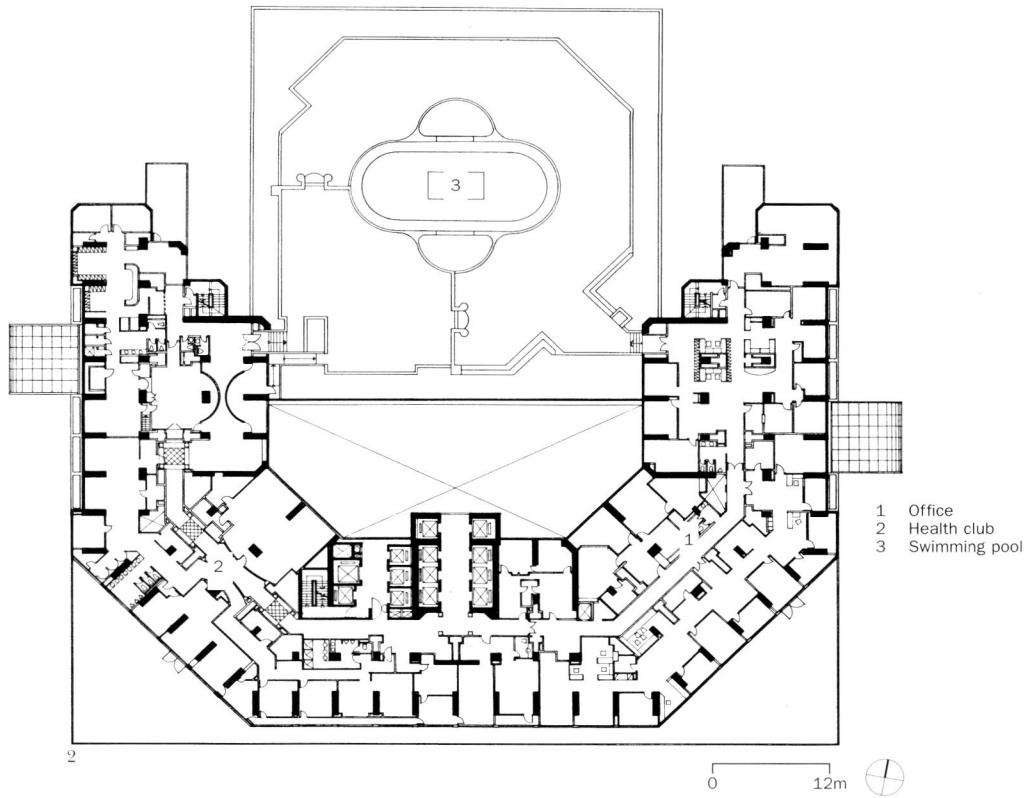

1 Office
2 Health club
3 Swimming pool

0   12m

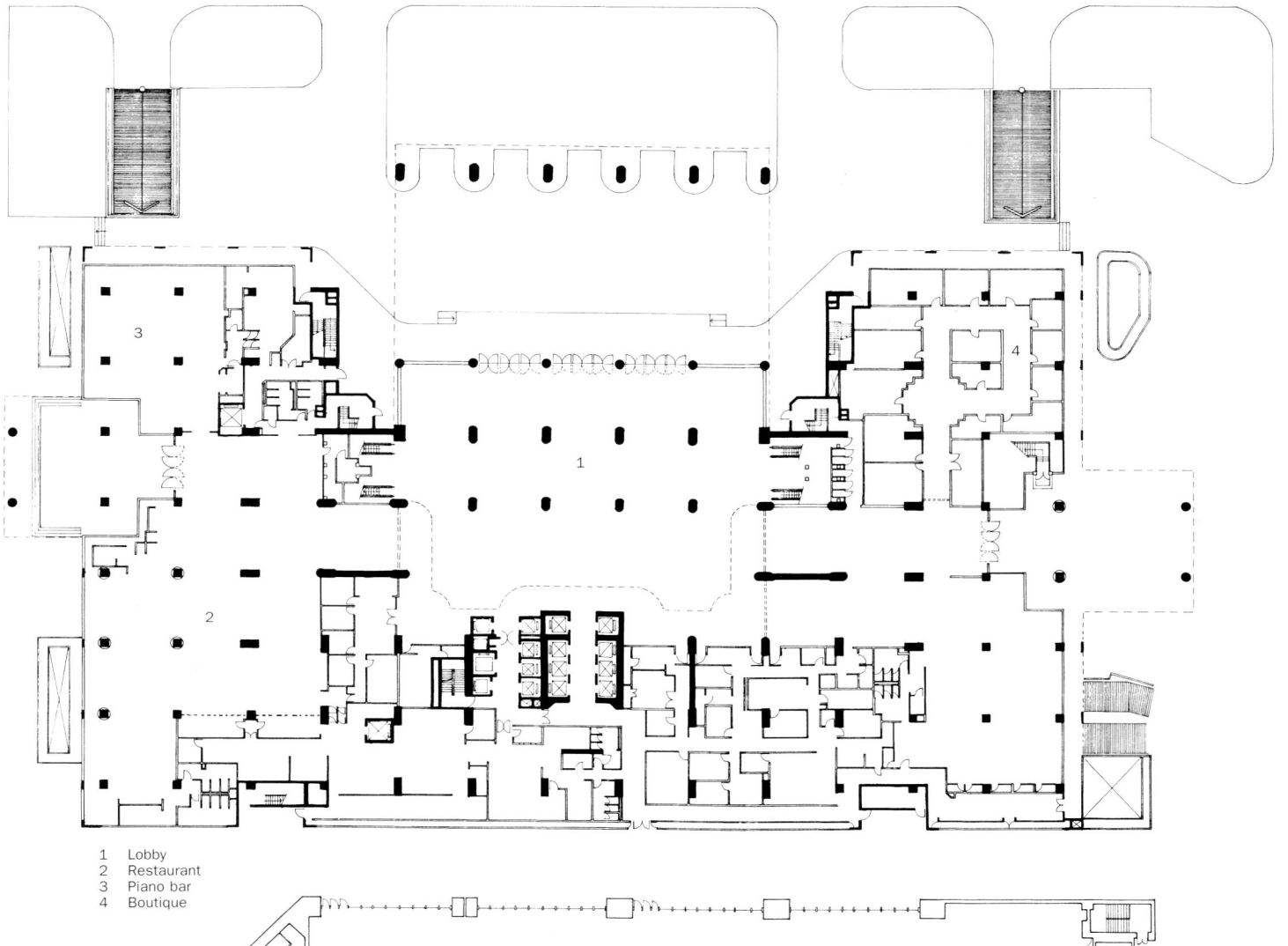

1 Lobby
2 Restaurant
3 Piano bar
4 Boutique

3

4   Cross section
5   View from the northeast
6   View from the north
7   Night view

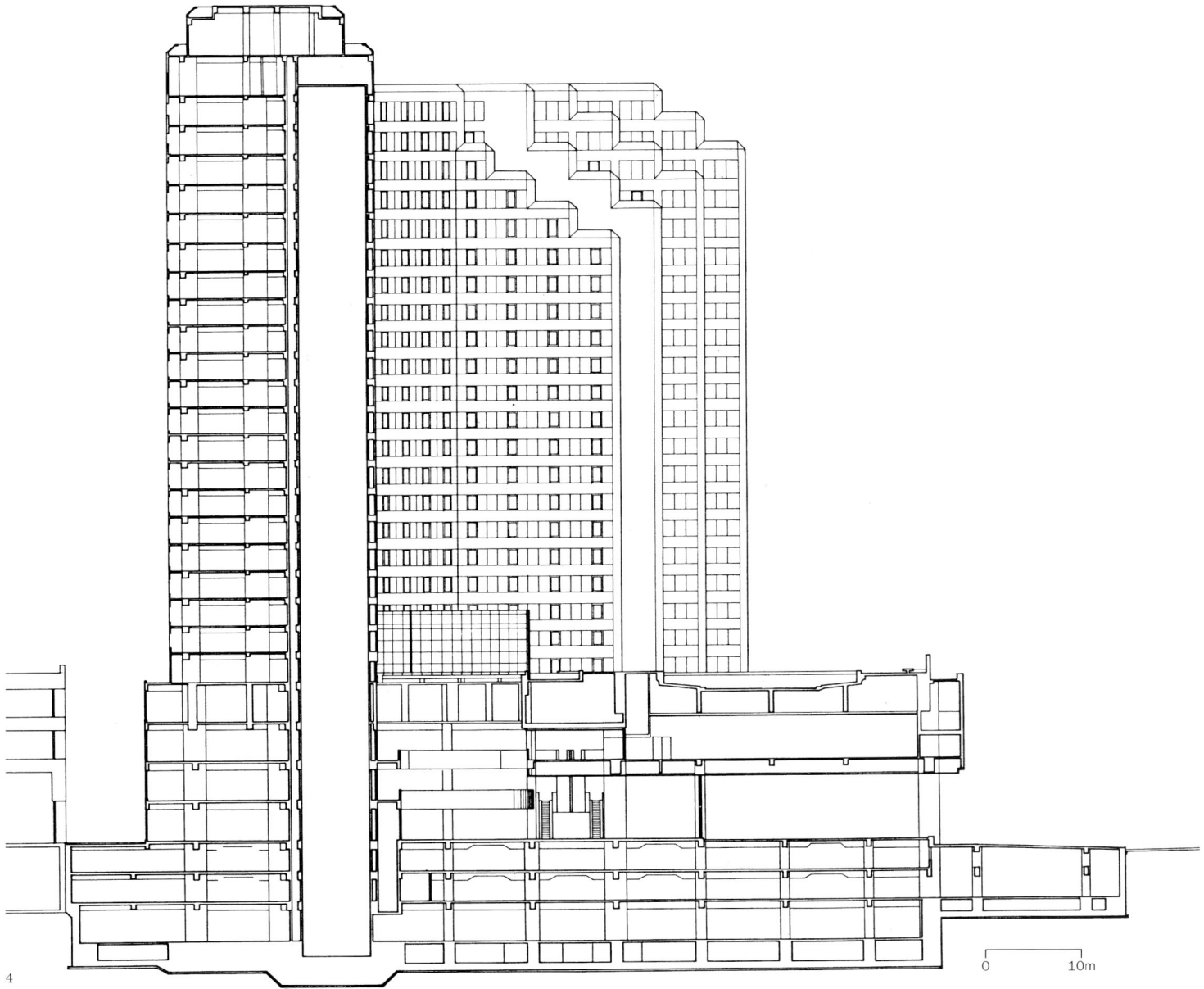

5

6

7

8 Partial view of main lobby
9 Main lobby

Emerald Rose Garden Hotel, Myanmar

Design/Completion 1994/2002
Rangoon, Myanmar
Emerald Rose Garden Hotel Co.
12,000 square meters
Reinforced concrete
Granite, sand stone and stucco

Although the Royal Rose Garden Hotel is in the heart of downtown Rangoon, it is adjacent to the forested area of the Burma Zoo. In the landscaped development of this 11-acre project, the design goal was to develop a serene garden featuring a swimming pool in the form of a forest lagoon, blending the hotel into the park-like setting of the zoo.

The architectural design of this project expresses local Myanmar traditions, both in the overall massing of the seven-story main building and in the details of the 350-room interior. Although this hotel provides accommodation at an international level, it also expresses its blending in with the local culture.

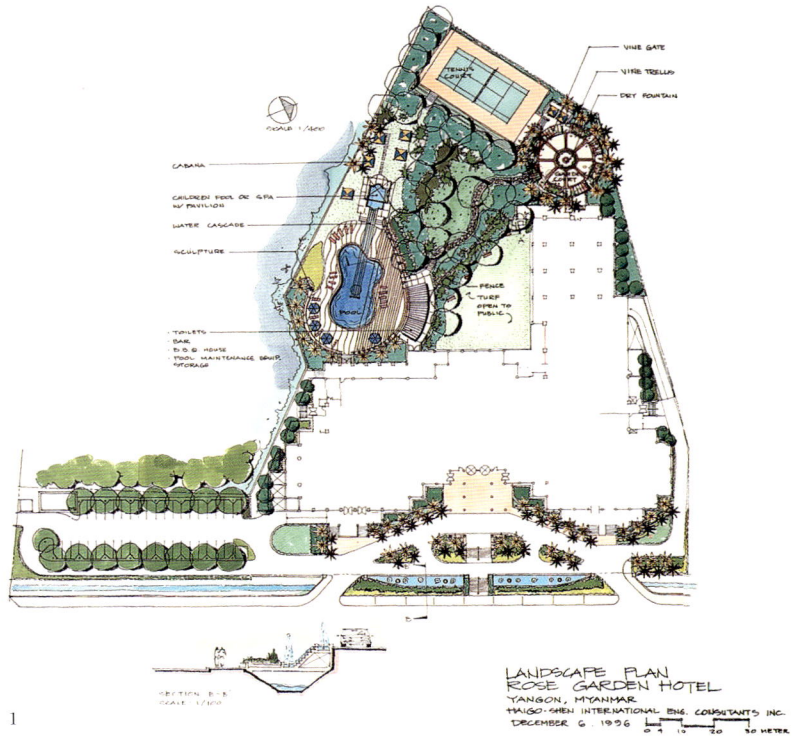

1

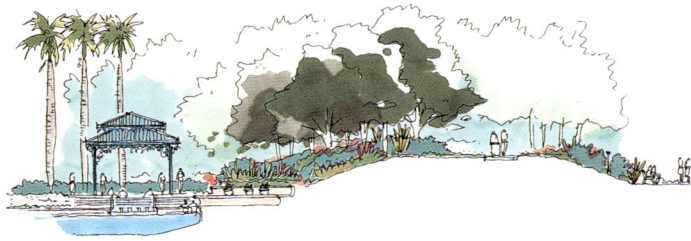

2

3

1   Landscape plan
2   Section of garden
3   Entrance porch
4   East elevation
5   Ground floor plan

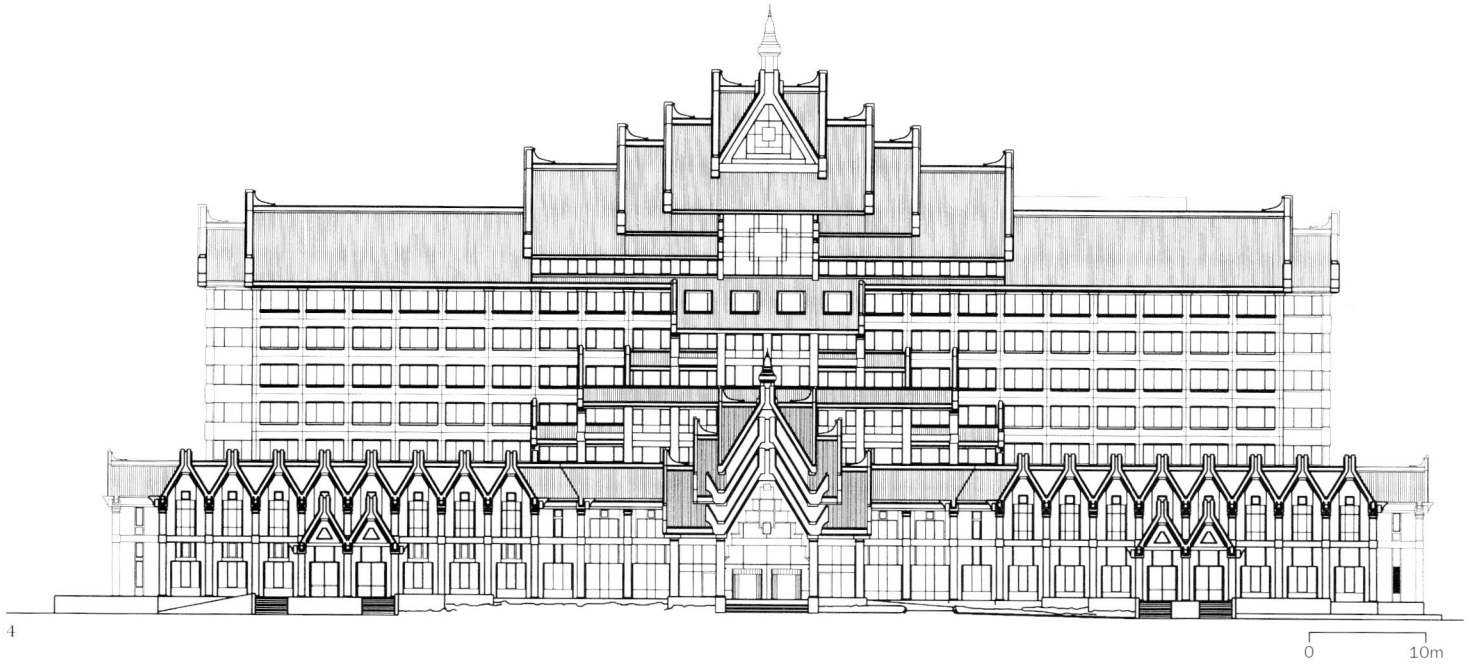

4

0   10m

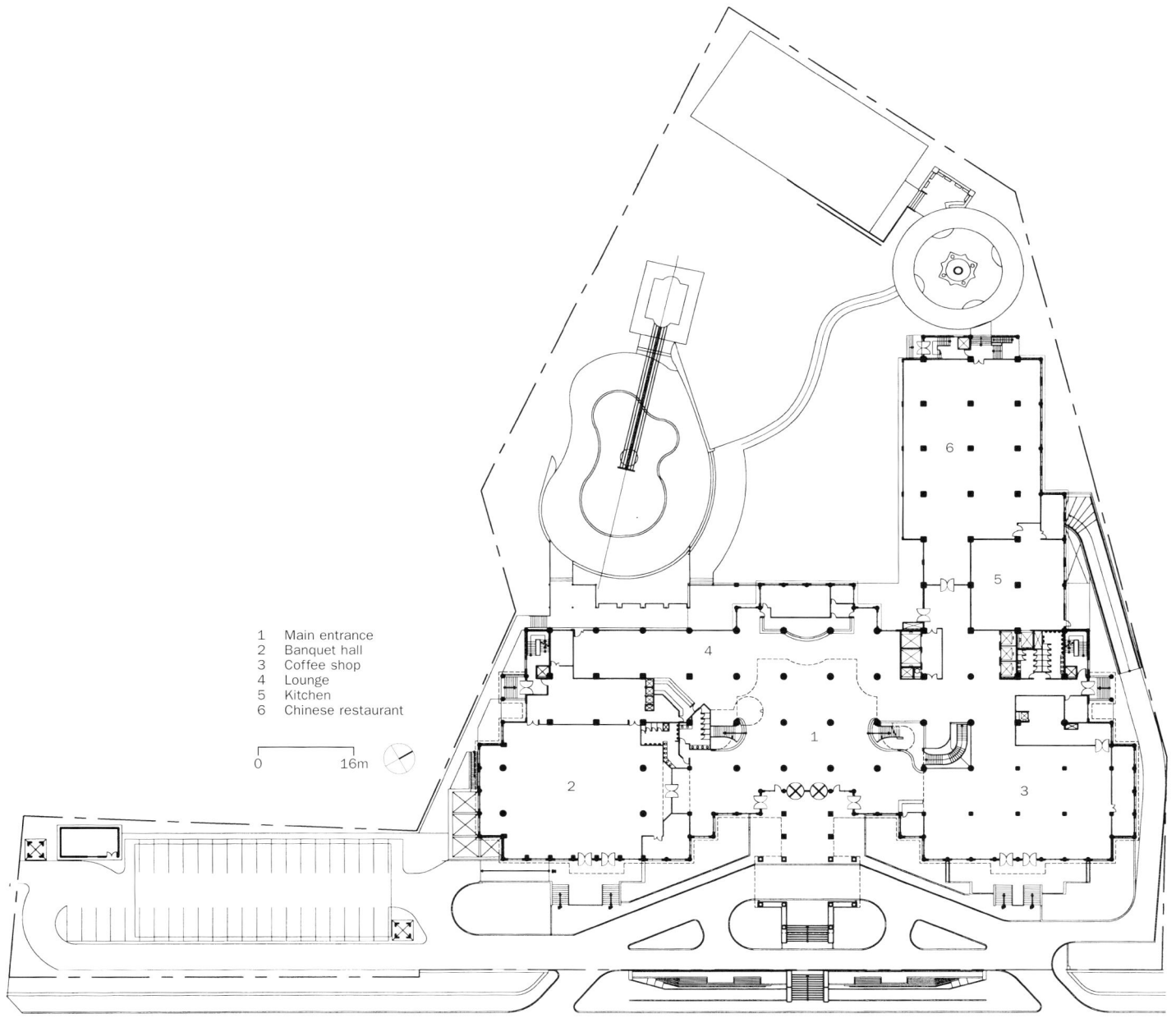

1 Main entrance
2 Banquet hall
3 Coffee shop
4 Lounge
5 Kitchen
6 Chinese restaurant

0   16m

5

Pan-German Motors Ltd, Headquarters

Design 1997
Taipei County, Taiwan
Pan-German Motors Ltd
14,086 square meters
B1—B2: steel, 1F–7F: reinforced concrete
Special heat-controlling glass with horizontal sun screens

The design objective of this project was, firstly, to express the advanced technology and high performance of the German automobiles marketed by this company from its new headquarters building, located in Tamshui, outside of Taipei. Accordingly, metal curtainwall panels were chosen for their similarity to automobile bodies, while the use of special heat-controlling glass with horizontal sun screens represents the use of technology to meet human needs, which is a hallmark of these automobiles.

This project also represents three aspects this client considered significant in its business methods: The use of curves in the building form introduces a more personal note to the design, emphasizing the attention to individualized customer service, as well as human interaction within the company. The tall windows of the first floor auto showroom allow customers to appreciate the scenery of the Tamshui River. The top-floor, multi-function meeting room was designed with a high degree of flexibility to provide for corporate activities such as presentation of new automobile models, ballroom dancing for employees, and other specialized activities.

Thus, the form of this building, together with its use of materials, responds in a unified way to technology, human interaction, the natural environment, and corporate business needs, providing the forward-looking direction requested by this client.

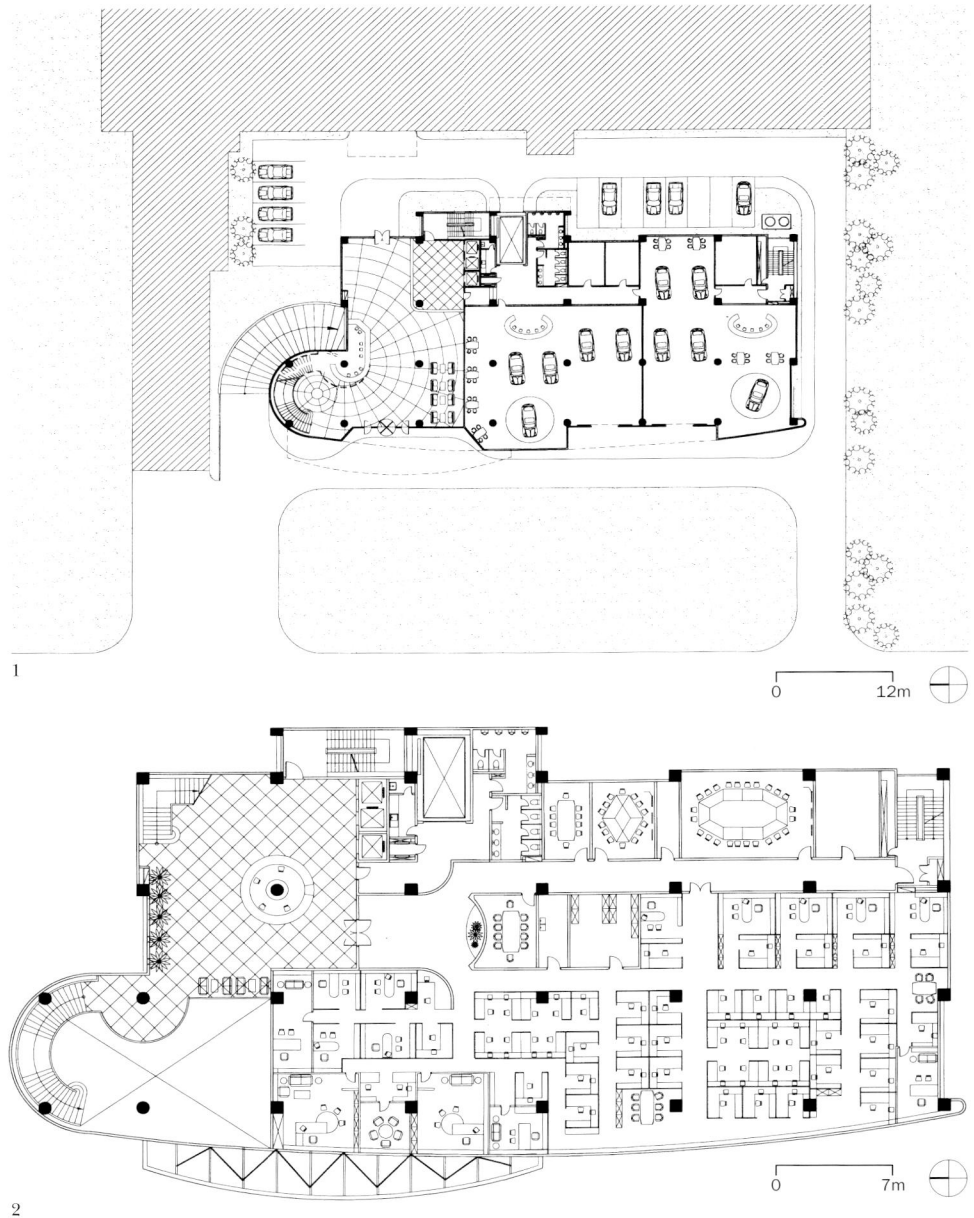

1

0   12m

2

0   7m

3

1   First floor plan
2   Second floor plan
3   Perspective

Nan Shan Corporation Headquarters

Design/Completion 1997/2003
Taipei, Taiwan
Nan Shan Life Insurance Co. Ltd
27,500 square meters
Steel structure
Granite and aluminium panel curtainwall
Joint-venture architect: C.F. Tong & Associates

Located in Taipei's Hsinyi Planning District, this site is part of the planned Asia Pacific Regional Financial Center. The client is the Taiwan affiliate of a multinational insurance and financial services firm.

Planning for this building is based on urban design factors, such as accommodation to neighboring buildings and open spaces, thus helping to create an harmonious urban environment. Designed according to human factors for both interior and exterior spaces, the process included wind-tunnel testing to ensure suitable microclimates for the exterior spaces.

The massing of the low and mid-rise portions of the tower use restrained and clean lines to express the safety and stability of this corporation, while also fulfilling the technical and economic requirements of a corporate office building. At the same time, the setbacks and transparent glazing on the corners of the high-rise portion of the tower enliven the skyline, creating a new landmark in the Hsinyi Special District.

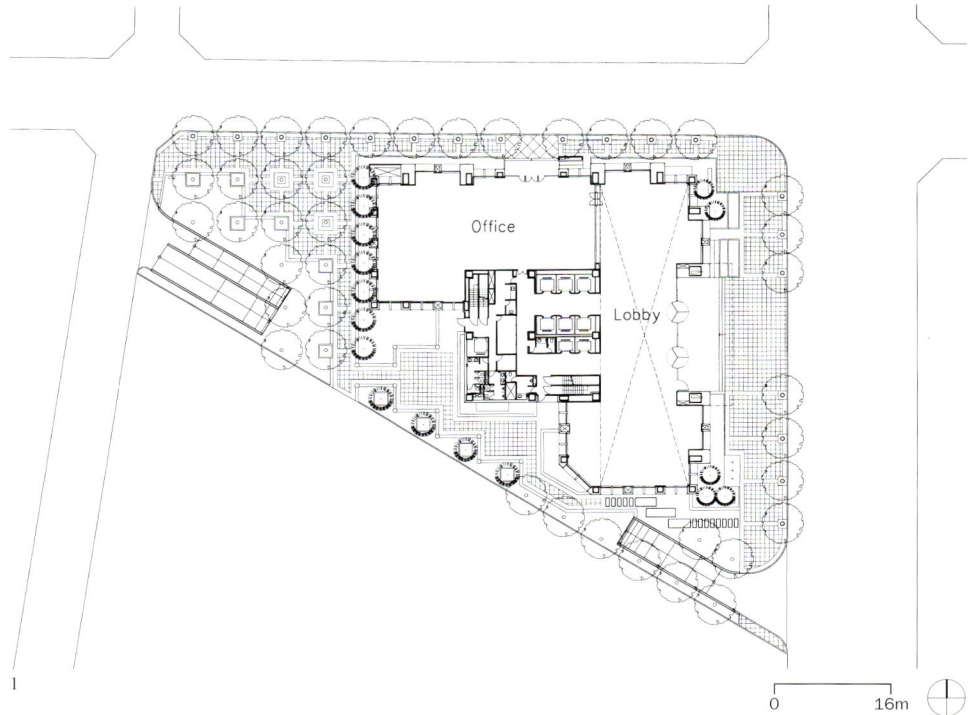

1   First floor plan
2   East elevation
3   North elevation
4   Perspective of night view

4

FE 21 Mega

Design/Completion 1995/2001 (Phase I)
Kaohsiung, Taiwan
Yuan-Ding Construction Co. Ltd
102,582.23 square meters (Phase I)
B2–B5: Reinforced concrete, B1: SRC, 1F–18F: Steel structure
Metal panel and glass curtainwall
Design Consultant: Wong & Ouyang Ltd, Hong Kong

Upon completion of the 103-story tower that is the centerpiece of the Asia Kaohsiung Plaza project as developed by the Far Eastern Group, it will be the tallest building in Taiwan, the second tallest in Asia, and the third tallest in the world. This landmark in Kaohsiung will mark the success of Taiwan's architectural, engineering, and construction abilities.

At a total cost approaching US$500 million, the project will be comprised of three major parts: an 18-story retail and entertainment center, a 40-story executive class hotel, and the 103-story office building. Overall construction is being phased sequentially over an 11-year period, beginning with the retail center.

The project team is coordinated by the Yuan-Ding Construction Company, with the Hong Kong architectural firm of Wang & Ouyang, Ltd providing exterior and preliminary design, and HSP responsible for the design development and construction supervision. The planning for this complex tries to integrate it into the Kaohsiung city fabric, including connections to the future subway system and a large green space and plaza with landscape design by HSP.

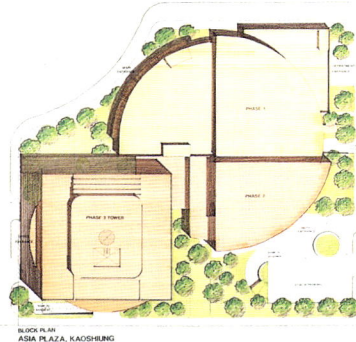

1

2

3

4

5

1   Site plan
2   First floor plan
3   East elevation of the retail and
    entertainment center
4   Rendering view from the northeast
5   Rendering view from the southeast
6   View from the southeast
7   View from the north
8   Night view of the plaza

6

7

8

9   Night view
10 Detail of the canopy
11 Food court

9

10

11

President International Tower

Design/Completion 1998/2004
Taipei, Taiwan
President Enterprises Group
123,000 square meters
Steel structure
Joint-venture firm: Kenzo Tange Associates, Japan

In consideration of President Enterprises Group's corporate image, the team introduced the concept of "the light tower towards the future." From this concept, a 40-story tower is situated on KeeLung Road where it is close to the main pedestrian traffic. With its uniform crystalline shape making all sides as its main elevation, this headquarters building is to be a focal point as well as a landmark building.

The interior space is organized mainly in two usage types. The lower levels are commercial facilities used for retail, and the higher levels are used for office spaces. Its typical floor plan mimics a perfect square, providing an easy layout interior.

The exterior form of the building uses setbacks at all four corners of the tower portion and repeats its setbacks once again at the upper level to create a prismatic sculpture that contributes to the interest and adds to the contrast of light and shadow on its elevation. The octagonal roof resembles a diamond mounted at the top of the tower; its function serves as a viewing platform to the city.

1   Aerial view
2   South elevation
3   Perspective from the southwest
4   Rendering for night view

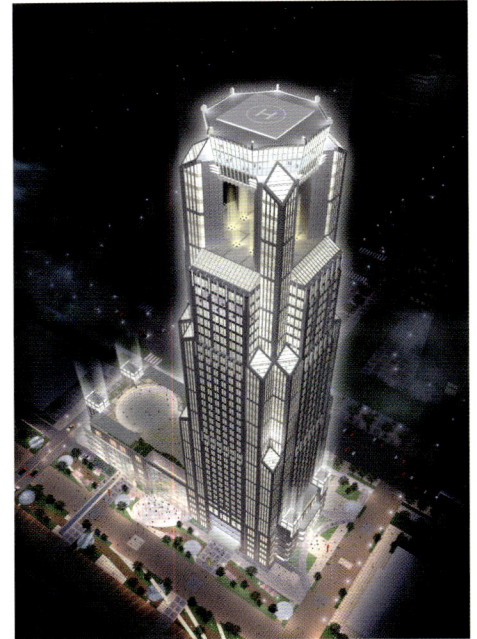

1

2

3

Recreation/Culture

National Museum of Marine Biology & Aquarium

Design/Completion 1990/2000(Phase I), 2001(Phase II)
Pingtung, Taiwan
National Museum of Marine Biology & Aquarium
26,179 square meters (Waters of Taiwan);
14,685 square meters (Coral Kingdom)
Mosaics and stones with reinforced concrete
Joint-venture firms: KCMI, USA; EHDD; J.J. Pan and Partners

Next to the ocean and within the Kenting National Park, this museum has three major exhibit themes: Waters of Taiwan, the Coral Kingdom, and Waters of the World. The facilities also include an independent entry hall, a research station, and a marine breeding center.

The Waters of Taiwan exhibit presents native aquatic ecologies, beginning from high mountain streams, passing through coastal marshes, and ending in the ocean itself. The Coral Kingdom uses deep-water materials, including a sunken ship and sea mammals. The two-story Waters of the World space offers visitors a view out to the coastline and the broader world of the oceans.

The building forms, designed with an international team of architects, engineering specialists, and museum designers, reflect the nature of the sea. The roofs of the exhibit halls have the rolling form of waves and the color scheme is graduated from a light aquamarine on the upper levels to a deep blue lower down, while the fountains and sculptures in the landscaping bring these themes to the exterior.

1

1 Night view from the sea
2 Night view
3 Ticket booth

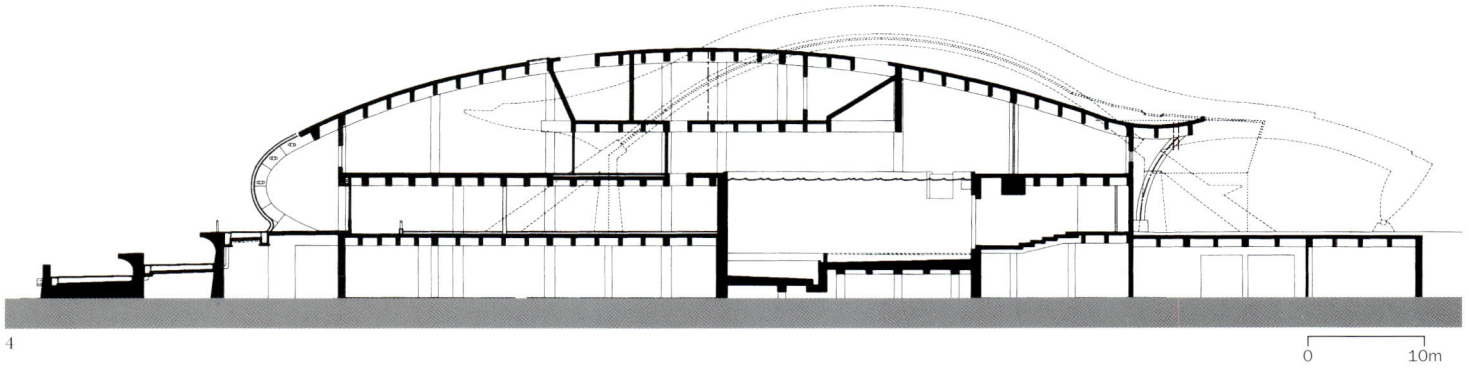

4

0　　　10m

5

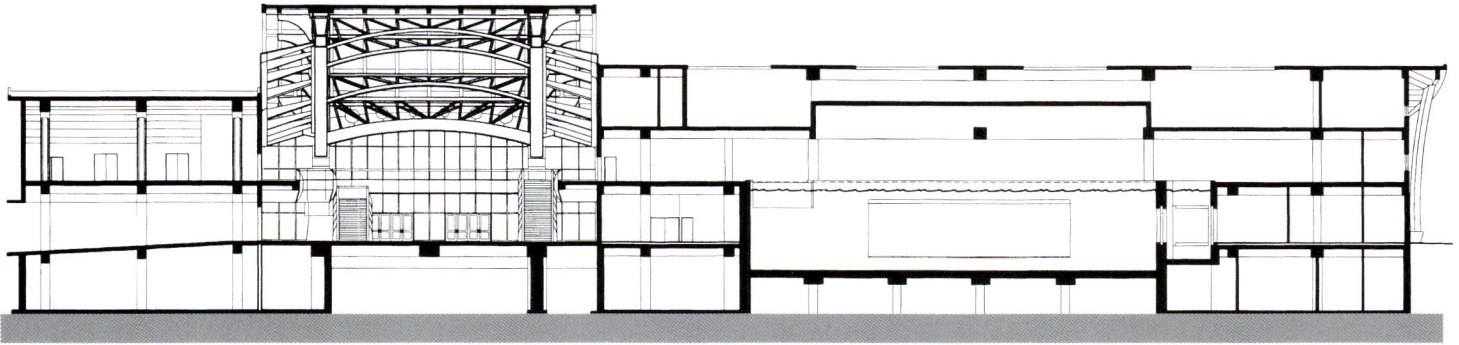

6

7

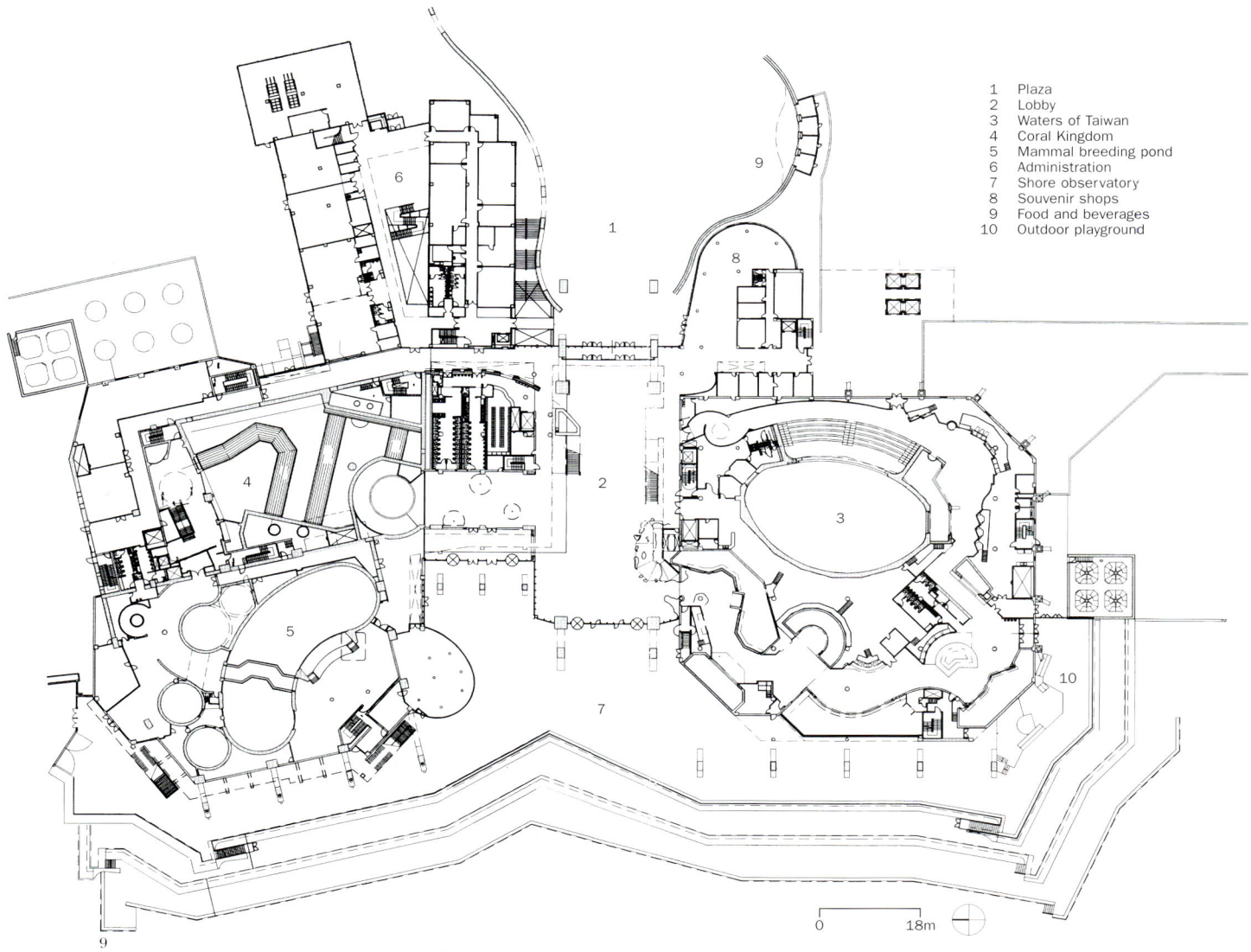

1 Plaza
2 Lobby
3 Waters of Taiwan
4 Coral Kingdom
5 Mammal breeding pond
6 Administration
7 Shore observatory
8 Souvenir shops
9 Food and beverages
10 Outdoor playground

0   18m

9   First floor plan
10 Shore observatory
11 Display area

12   Main lobby
13   Third floor plan
14   Administrative area atrium
15   Waters of Taiwan viewing area

12

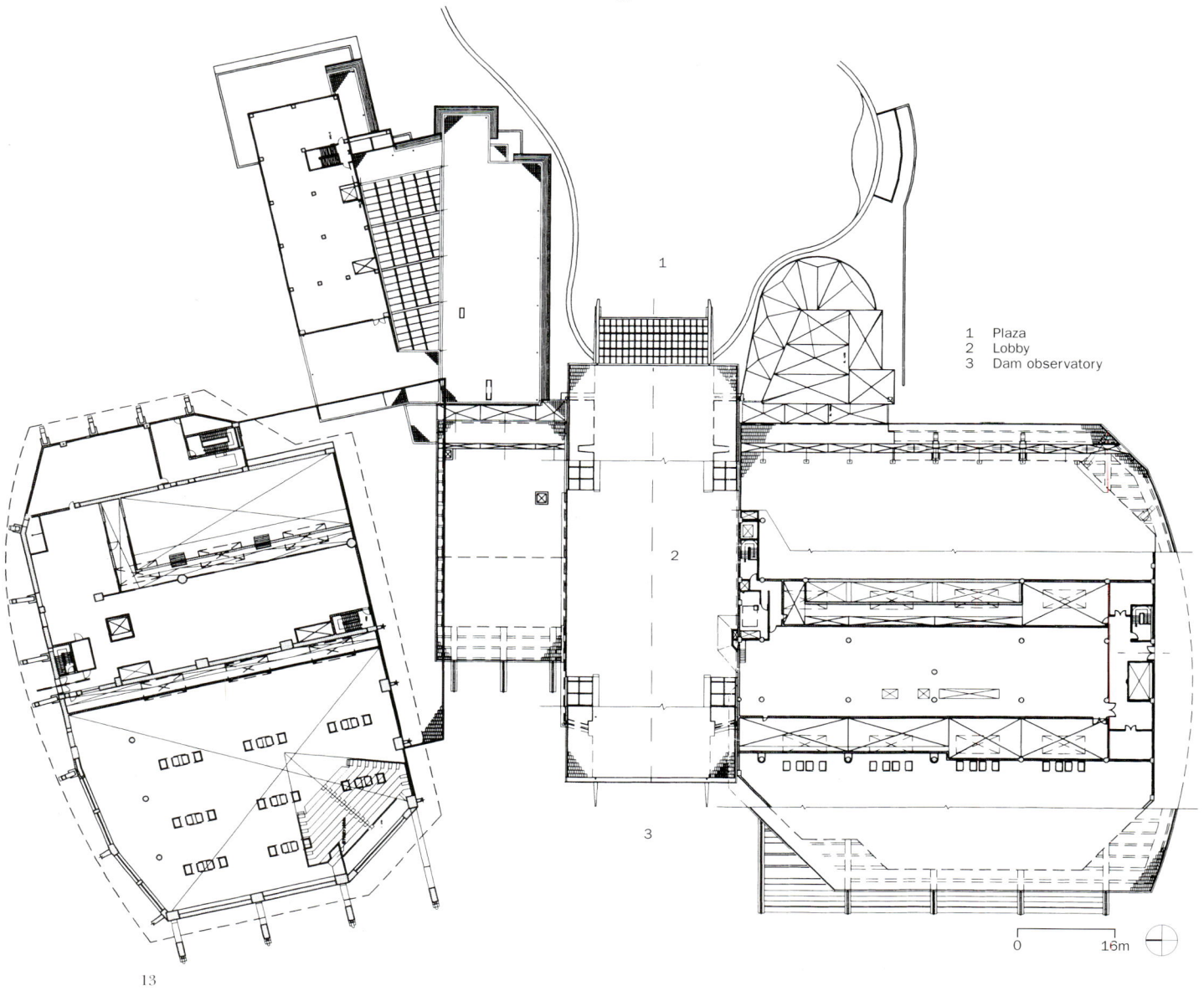

1   Plaza
2   Lobby
3   Dam observatory

1

2

3

0   16m

13

14

15

Yamay Discovery World Water Park

Design/Completion 1999/2000
Taichung, Taiwan
Yamay International Development Co. Ltd
72,840 square meters

Located in Taichung county, the $25 billion Yamay water theme park sits on 200 acres consisting of three zones, namely the central multi-recreational zone, the family recreational zone on the west side, and the leisure zone on the east side. The site will be developed in three separate phases and will be completed in 10 years' time. Our office is involved in its first phase, covering 72,840 square meters including Malabay water park, theme restaurant, and employees' building.

The overall concept is to create an unprecedented and comprehensive water theme park. Once in the park, visitors could experience the wonders of Taiwanese tradition and local culture. Other design goals are to create a theme park with international standards and to make it the most distinctive multifunctional recreational resort in the nation.

1

2

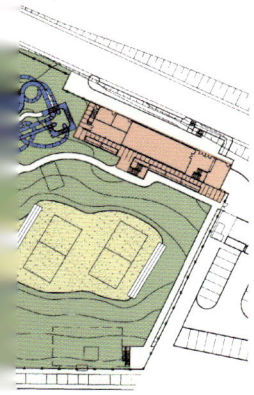

30m

3

4   Activity pool
5   Artificial wave swimming pool
6   Changing room building

4

5

6

National Museum of Prehistory

Design/Completion 1993/2001
Taitung, Taiwan
National Museum of Prehistory
Joint-venture firm: Michael Graves & Associates,
the SWA Group (Landscape)
47,525 square meters
Reinforced concrete
Tile and stone exterior

On a site outside of Taitung, this museum is dedicated to preserving and displaying the history of early Taiwanese cultures, as well as illustrating the development of humankind in other areas of the world. In addition to exhibition galleries, the complex includes an international conference facility, administration offices, a library, curatorial laboratories, and archival storage, as well as housing for scholars. The site has been designed as public park, using themes from the native landscape to evoke the feeling of prehistoric environments.

The design was prepared in collaboration with the American firm Michael Graves & Associates, and was the winner of an international design competition. Arranged around a central courtyard for performances, the buildings of the complex create an axis extending to the mountain ranges beyond, integrating the architecture with the natural landscape. The building façades have the tile and stone used in traditional architecture, and also incorporate motifs from indigenous peoples, imbuing the project with a true regional spirit.

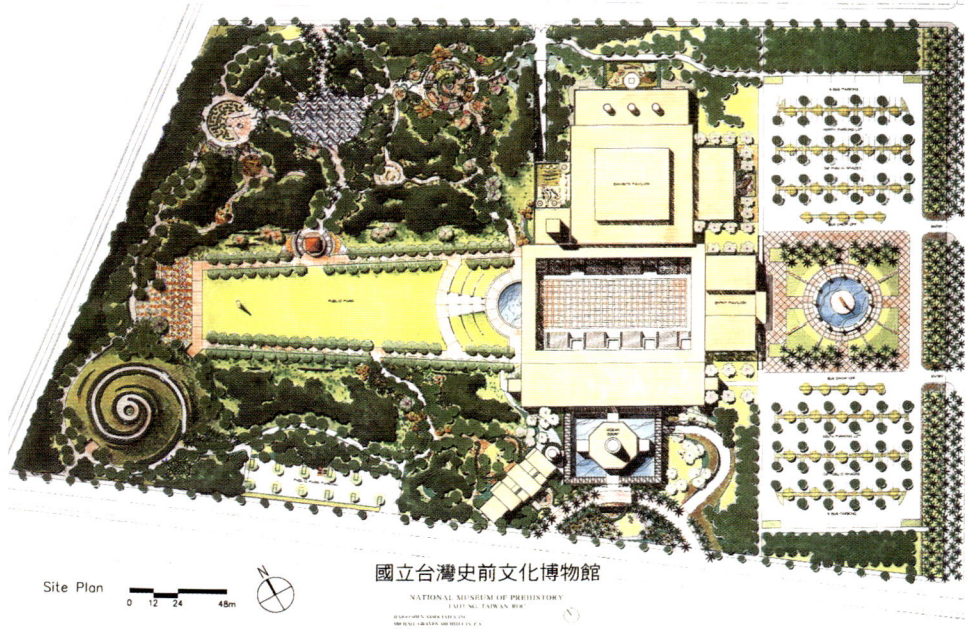

國立台灣史前文化博物館

Site Plan
0 12 24   48m

1

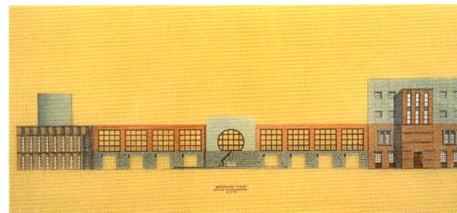

2

3

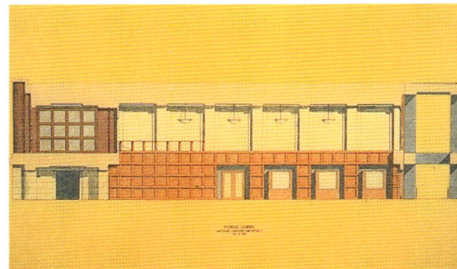

4

5

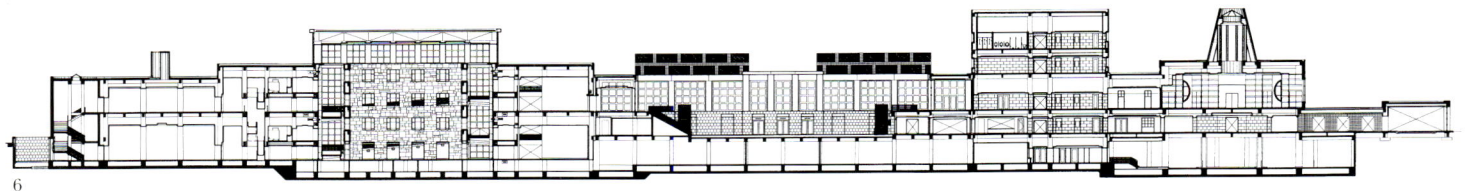

6

1   Site plan
2   West elevation
3   Elevation of the main entrance
4   Interior elevation of the entry pavilion
5   North elevation of the exhibits pavilion
6   Longitudinal section
7   Model from the east
8   Model from the south
9   Site aerial view

7

8

9

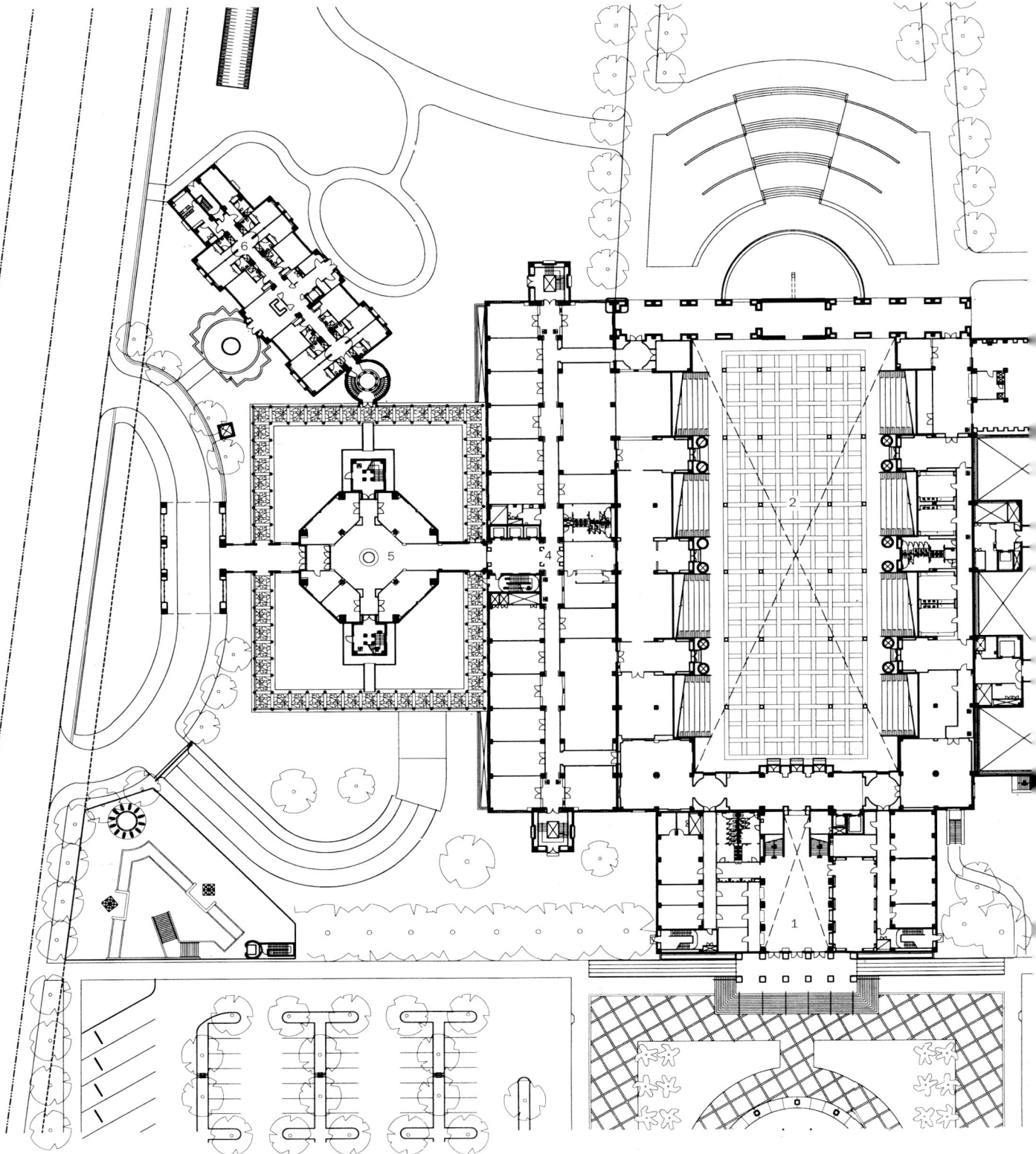

10

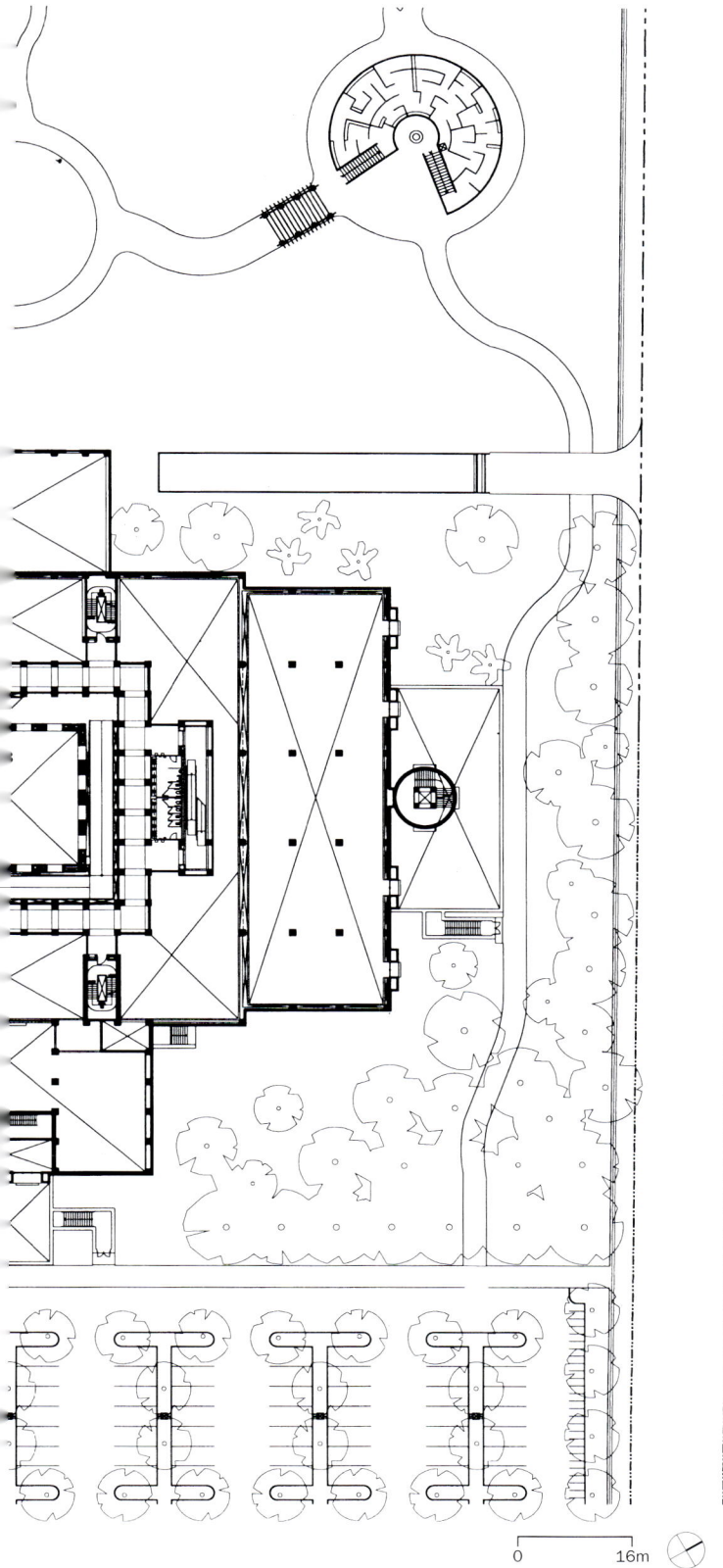

0   16m

11

12

13

14

15 Open colonnade looking to central courtyard
16 View from the north

The National Museum of Taiwan History, Tainan

Design (Competition) 2001
Tainan, Taiwan
15,100 square meters
Steel structure
Precast PC panel and curtainwall
Joint-venture firm: Kisho Kurokawa Architect & Associates, Japan

The overall concept of the design is to organize the outdoor and indoor spaces in an orderly manner. The vast entrance plaza features a theme depicting the 24 seasons of the lunar calendar. It leads to the main exhibition pavilions, which have different themes focusing on the people, land, and culture of Taiwan history. Visitors will then experience an outdoor park designed as a collage of an abstract version of the gradually disappearing farmlands, fishponds, sugar-cane fields, and salt lakes. The texture of this rich landscape provides the context for the layout of the museum.

The form of the building symbolizes the abstract form of a flying egret, a native bird, and people are identified with the land. The buildings are divided into two major parts on the first floor: the public areas and the collection and research areas. The entrance lobby, with a 6-meter-high space, will be the focal point for display of major pieces of the theme exhibition. There are spaces for restaurants and souvenir shops, and outdoor exhibition areas with separate entrances. The second floor is the paid area. It consists of the main exhibition rooms. The museum library and education rooms are also located on this floor. The third floor is the area of administrative functions, such as the director's and deputy directors' offices, general office space, and service facilities.

The design of the interior space is to dramatize the space sequence with a self-identified central space as the focal point, a transitional space linking different self-contained spaces. It also gives an overall holistic feeling. In the meanwhile, each pavilion will be designed with different characteristics, according to its function.

1

2

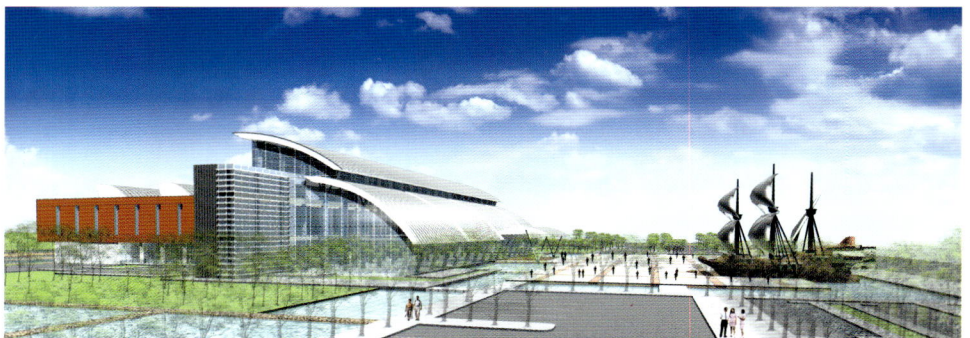

3

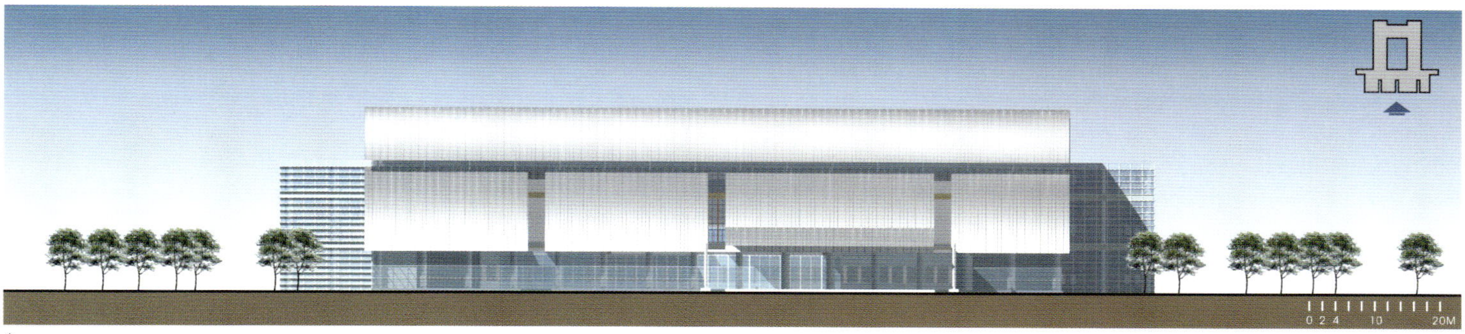

4

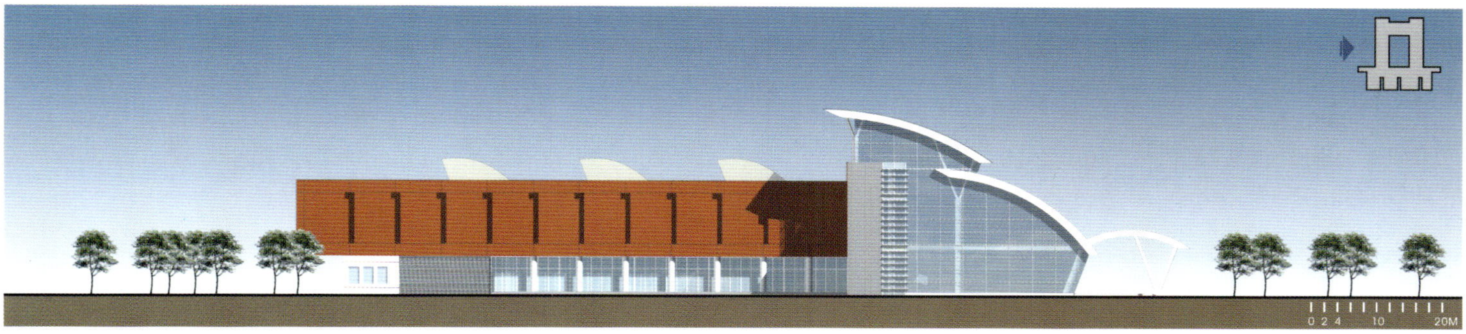

5

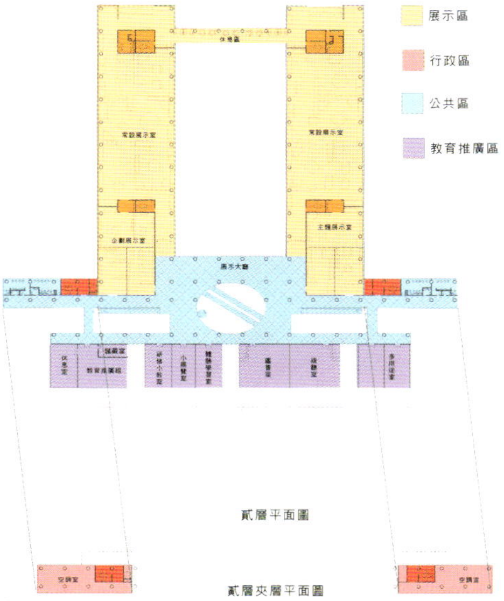

展示區
行政區
公共區
教育推廣區

貳層平面圖

貳層夾層平面圖

6

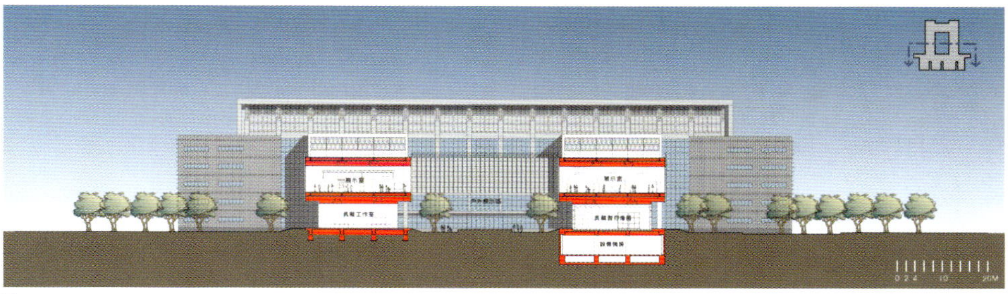

7

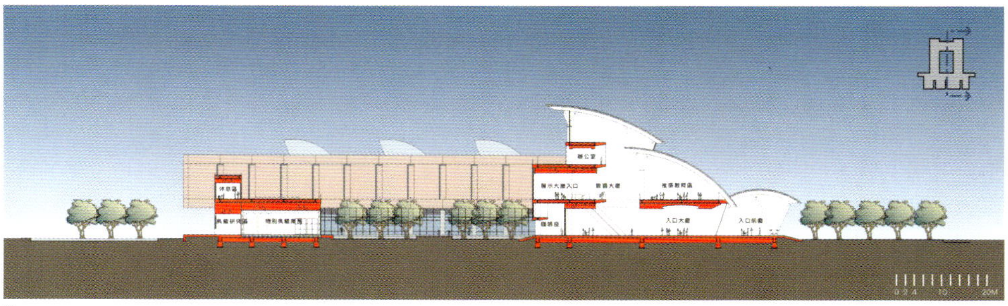

8

1 Site plan
2 Aerial rendering
3 View of entrance
4&5 Elevations
6 Second floor plan
7&8 Sections

Ocean Park and Farest Resort, Hualien

Design/Completion 1997/2002
Hualien, Taiwan
Metropolitan Construction Co. Ltd
Joint-venture firms: Weathered House Pty Ltd (General Consultant),
Alan Griffith (Architect) Pty Ltd
(Overall site conceptual design and the specialist
design architect for the Marine Park)
Resort hotel: Wimberly Allison Tong & Goo
Overall site area: 45 hectares
Theme park (Zone A): 14 hectares
Resort hotel (Zone B): 45,000 square meters

The Hualien Ocean Park resort development is located north of Hualien, on the shore of the Pacific Ocean, with the mountains of the Eastern Coastal Range rising at the back of the site. The project is significant not only for the natural beauty of its site, located adjacent to the East Coast National Scenic District, but also for its role in the government's goal of attracting development to the eastern part of Taiwan. Accordingly, the planning and design meets international standards for tourist accommodation.

On this project, Haigo Shen & Partners is the local architect part of an international team of developers, architects, and landscape designers, in addition to being responsible for interior design. The 45-hectare site is planned in three districts: the amusement park itself, a natural scenic district, and the 438-room resort hotel complex. Although each area has its own distinct character, the entire complex is designed so that visitors are led from one area to another, accomplishing the joint goals of education, recreation, and relaxation, in the context of environmentally responsible development.

1

1 Overall site plan
2 Site model
3 Arrival zone elevation
4 Ocean park master plan
5 Aerial view of resort hotel

2

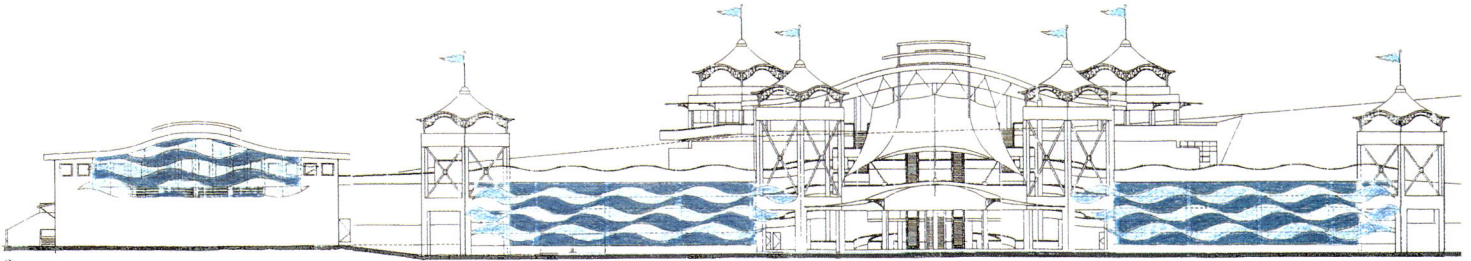

3

4

5

6 Main street elevation
7 Club house
8 Resort hotel garden

COLORBOND CUSTOM ORB.
ROOF SHEETING
鋭街層頂
GLAZING IN POWDERKOTE ALUMINIUM
JOINERY
隔面銀玻璃鋁窗

COLORBOND CUSTOM ORB
ROOF SHEETING ON
STEEL FRAME.
鈑翠硬玻屋頂

6

7

8

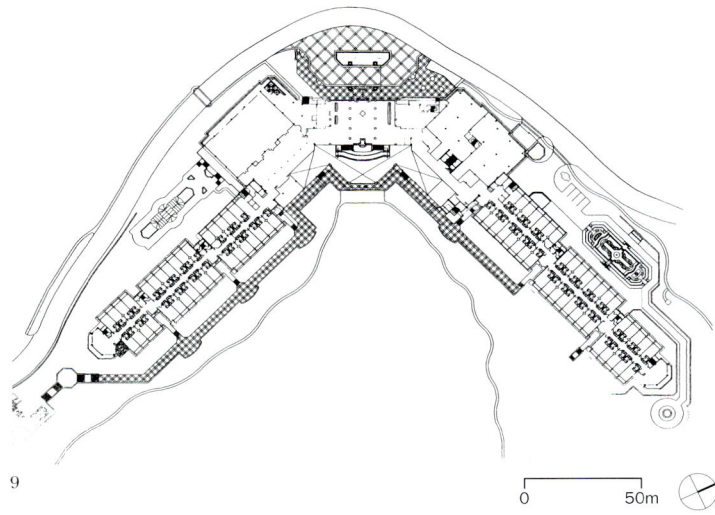

9

0   50m

10

Kaohsiung Arena

Design (Competition) 1994
Kaohsiung, Taiwan
Kaohsiung City Government
100,068 square meters
Reinforced concrete, roof with steel structure

The design concept behind the Kaohsiung Arena is not only to create a modern, 21st-century arena, but also an unique building representing the city of Kaohsiung.

The design principles are:

Representing Kaohsiung, a Harbor City
The exterior styling of the Kaohsiung Arena mimics the bow of a grand ship, and with its exposed structure—much like cargo lifts by the harbor—presents an image that is true to the unique qualities of Kaohsiung's industrial harbor. The strength and beauty of the arena is accentuated through the aerodynamic shapes of its architecture.

Layers of Visual Differentiation
From afar, the overall styling of the arena is well distinguished. Up close, its details are friendly to the eye.

Humanized Scale
Usually, a massive building structure creates a distant feeling for its occupants; therefore, the arena is designed in layers of volume. Changes in materials and shifts in its details help to create a place that is friendlier to the people. Multiple focal points provide an architecture that is energetic and full of life.

With the combination of architecture and imagery, using high-tech electronic viewing screens and communications equipment, an arena that reflects a time of the future is being presented.

1

2

128

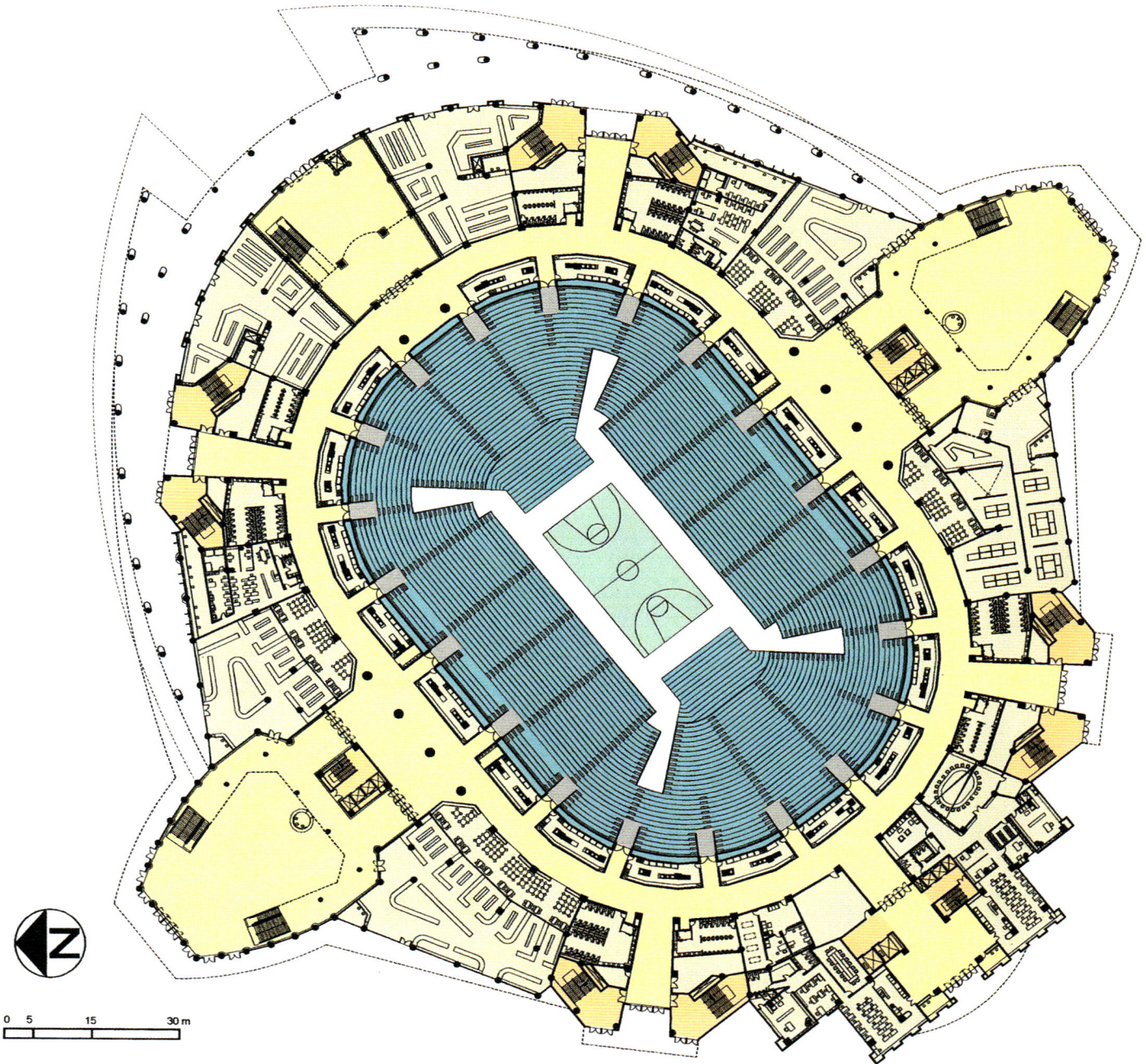

1 Site plan
2 Perspective from the north
3 First floor plan

0 5   15   30 m

3

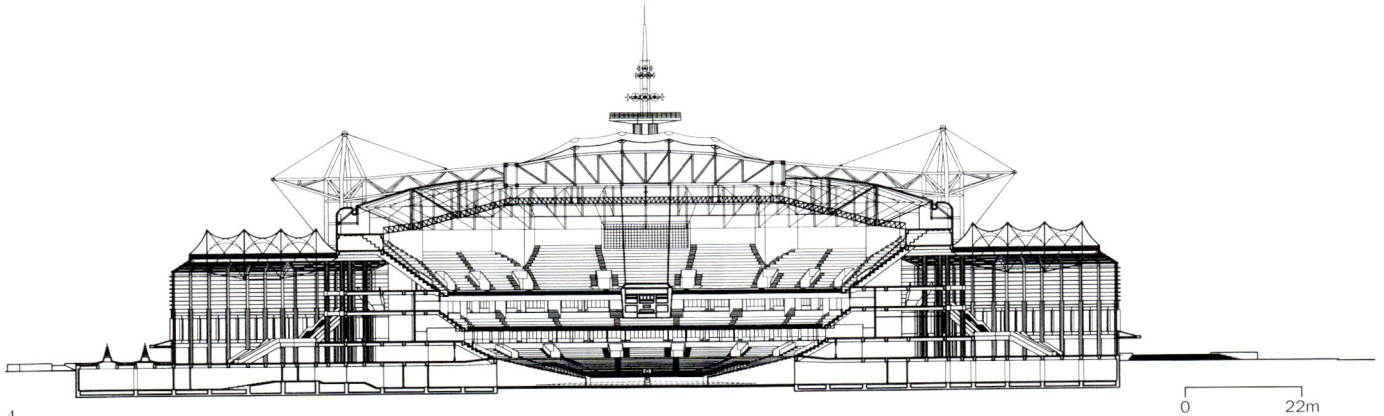

4

0 22m

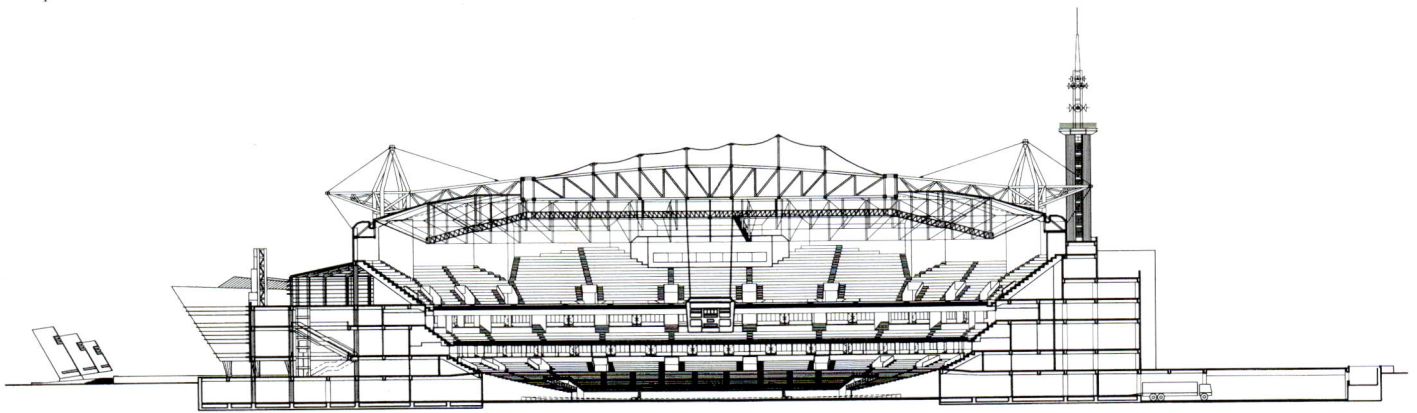

5

4   Longitudinal section
5   Cross section
6   Perspective from the east
7   North elevation
8   East elevation

6

7

8

Baseball Stadium, Kaohsiung

Design (Competition) 1995
Kaohsiung, Taiwan
Kaohsiung City Government
Reinforced concrete, roof with steel structure

The Kaohsiung baseball stadium is a modern stadium able to host baseball games at international standard. It can accommodate 25,000 spectators. The stadium will become a major recreational and leisure location for people in Kaohsiung. The aim in designing such a ballpark is to have an international and modern baseball stadium that is self-sufficient and multi-functional.

The stadium was designed on the idea of smooth lines, in order to emphasize the importance of smoothness in architectural design for sport purposes. With this idea in mind, this stadium provides spectators with the largest number of good seats. Vertical lines and good services are emphasised by this ballpark.

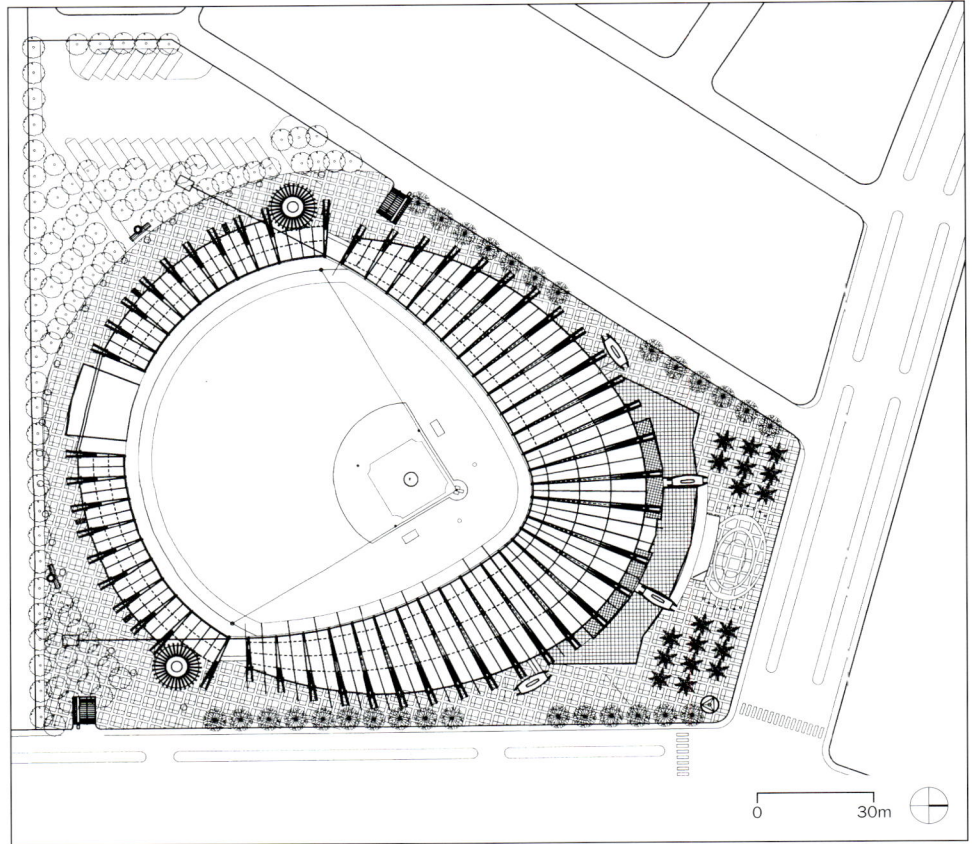

1

0   30m

1   Site plan
2   Longitudinal section
3   First floor plan
4   View from seat

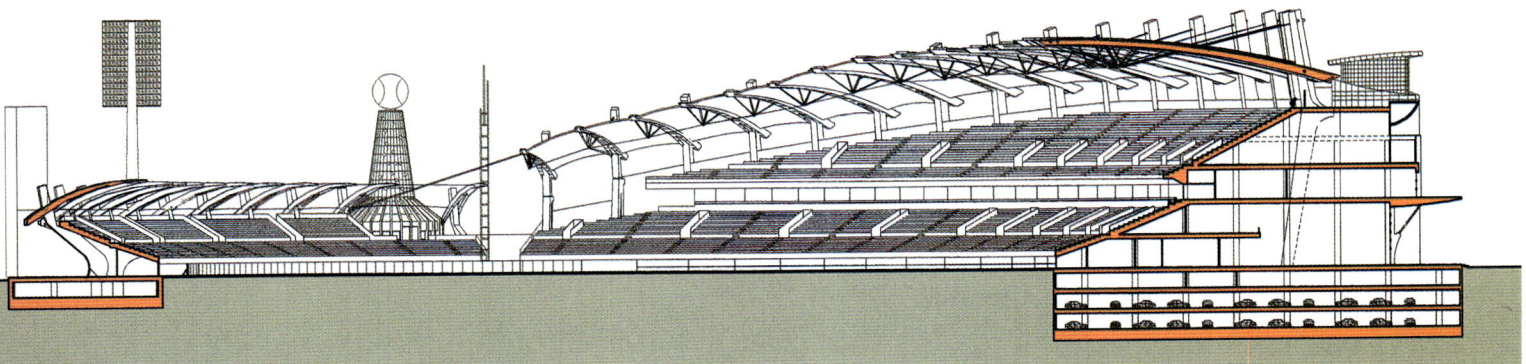

2

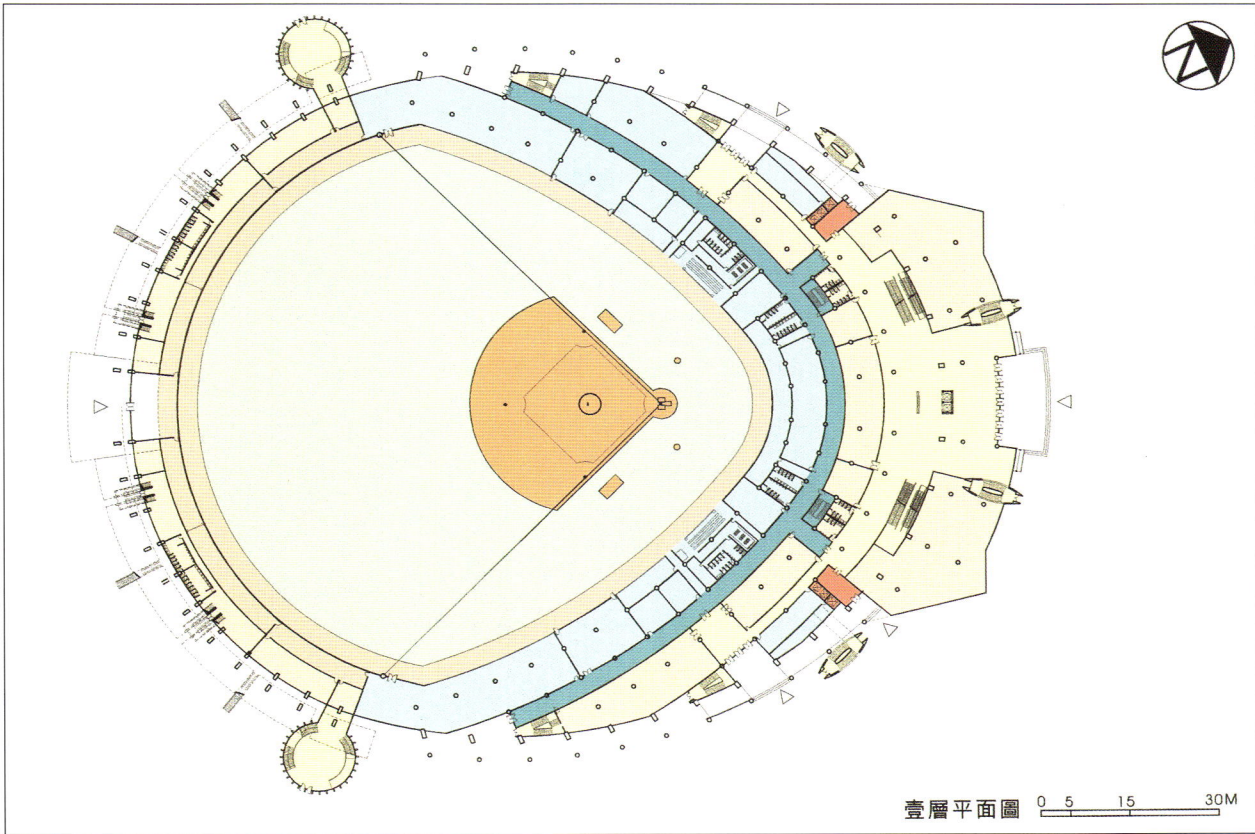

壹層平面圖　0　5　15　30M

3

4

5

Transportation

Taipei Main Station

Design/Completion 1984/1989
Taipei, Taiwan
Engineering Office of Taipei Railway Underground Project, Ministry of
Transportation and Communications
175,000 square meters
Tile with reinforced concrete
Joint-venture firms: C.K. Chen Architect, KMG Architect/Japan

This station is the key to the urban infrastructure improvement project of placing underground the main railway line which runs through downtown Taipei. Similarly, the planning of the station worked to knit together the urban street pattern of the western commercial districts of the city. This station, which was the first underground railway project in Taiwan, was designed to act as the central hub in Taipei's urban mass transportation network, providing connections to many other modes of transportation.

The Taipei Main Station is a huge project; with six levels above ground and four under ground, it uses its roof and other forms to create a traditional Chinese style in a modern idiom, giving a sense of local identity to this national landmark. Inside, there is a tall and bright space for the passenger ticket center, where departing passengers can purchase tickets and then easily move by escalators to waiting halls on the sides of the building, which connect to the train platforms. Arriving passengers can move quickly to other modes of mass transportation or to parking garages. In their movement and while they wait, passengers are also offered other facilities, such as an art gallery and shops. Apart from the provisions for passengers, this building houses a complex of administrative offices on the upper levels, which have their own separate entrances and circulation.

The design of this grand terminal successfully solves a program which is technically and functionally complex, at the same time providing a building that is a vital part of many people's image of modern Taipei.

1   Aerial view

1

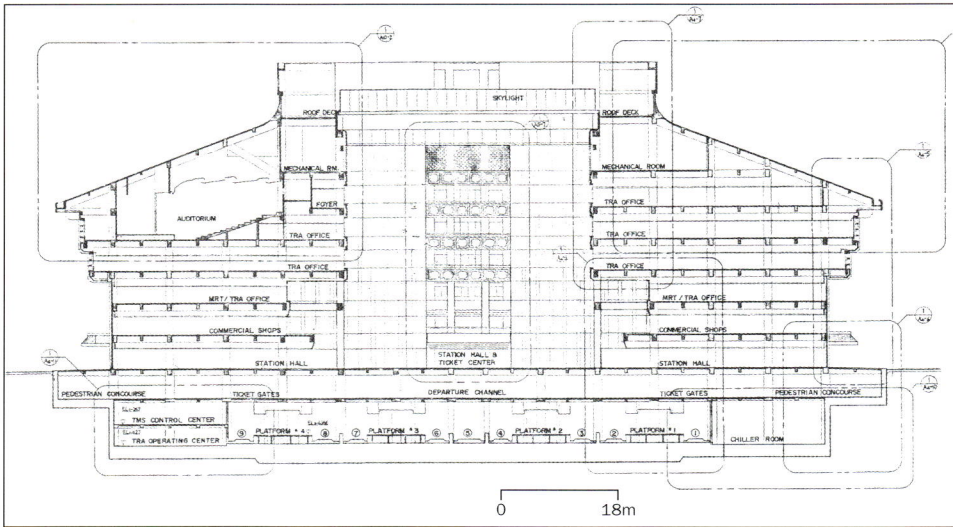

2

3

4

5

6

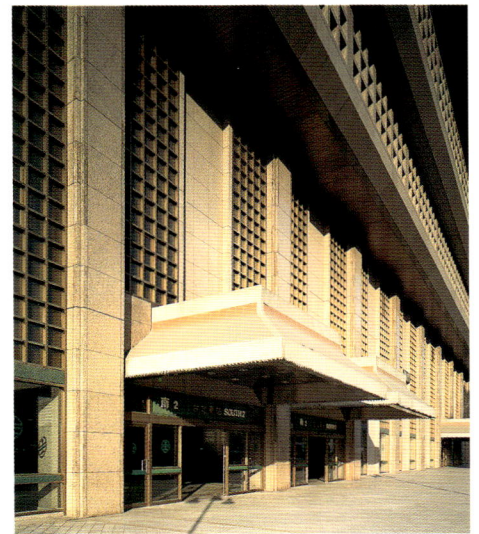

7

Terminal Building, Taipei International Airport

Design/Completion 1969/1971
Taipei, Taiwan
Civil Aeronautic Administration
40,720 square meters
Reinforced concrete
Joint-venture firms: C.K. Chen & Associates, Da-Hong Wong & Associates

Taipei Sung-Shan (International) Airport is situated at the northern end of the boulevard of Tun-Hua North Road. The airport is currently the pivot of domestic aviation. However, when this project was completed in 1971, Sung-Shan Airport was still the main international airport as well as the domestic airport for Taiwan. It was the gateway to Taiwan—a very important position.

The air terminal occupies a total space of more than 40,000 square meters. With an elegant vertical square design, it has blended traditional Chinese architecture with a sense of modernization. The high-rising pillars support the two layers of beams and stretch the beams to project out into a vertical design element. The design offers a hint of a wooden house framework structure; simple, but powerful. The arc-shaped roof, ornamented with gorgeous yellow tiles, makes it easy to relate it to the traditional construction of the imperial palace. The double-roofing design with a spout gives a sense of rhythm. Overall, this building properly conveys the symbolic meaning of making the Sung-Shan Airport the gateway to the country, with an image of solemnity and elegance.

1

2

1 Front façade
2 View from the northeast
3 Departure lobby
4 Porch

MCTS Transit Station, Taipei

Design/Completion 1988/1996
Taipei, Taiwan
Department of Rapid Transit System, Taipei City Government
Joint-venture firms: T.Y. Lin Taiwan Inc., MATRA Inc.
102,476 square meters (12 stations)
Steel structure

The MRT Mucha Line has a total of 12 stations. In order to reflect the integration and variety of the line, the complex, multi-functional station was divided into several construction components. Each component could be brought together according to the needs of each station. The design concept of each component is as follows:

Platform: in order to create the gracefulness of the entire station design, "walkways" and "bowed roof" designs used in Chinese architecture were applied, so that there are no sharp edges or protruding lines on the platform, while the size of the main construction is reduced to a minimum.

Elevator: An elevator for the physically impaired is installed in each station. A cage-like safety glass panel was designed and placed at both ends of the platform, creating a "lantern" effect at the stations' designed entrance/exit gates.

Escalator, stairwells: These provide the vertical motion lines of the station as well as the largest construction component aside from the station platform. Their design is modified according to the different surroundings.

1

2

3

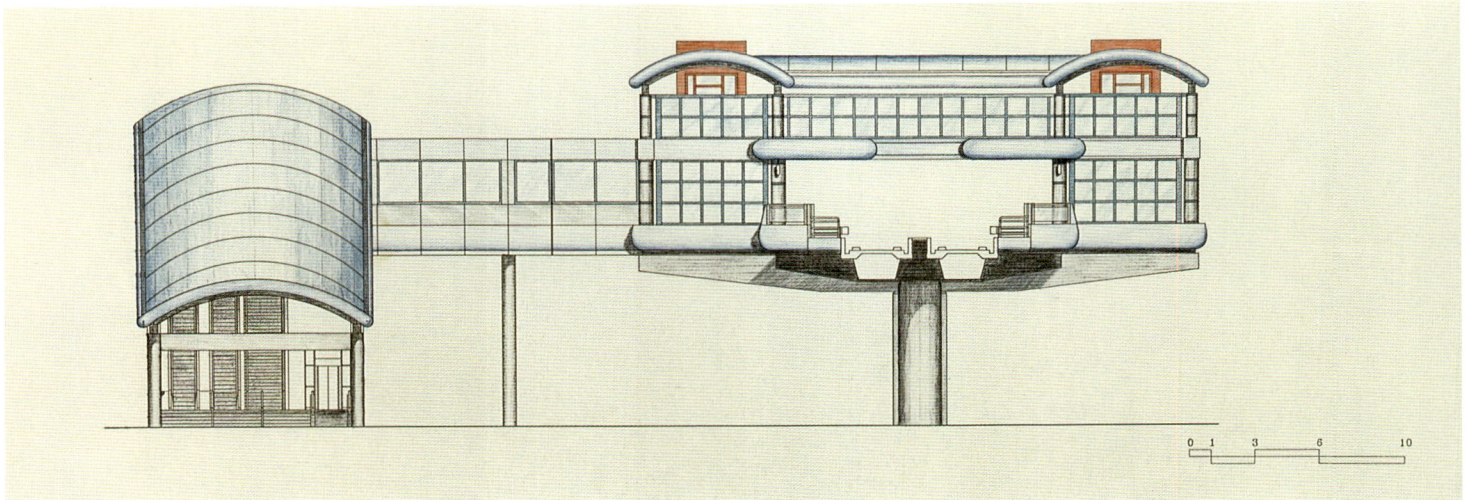

4

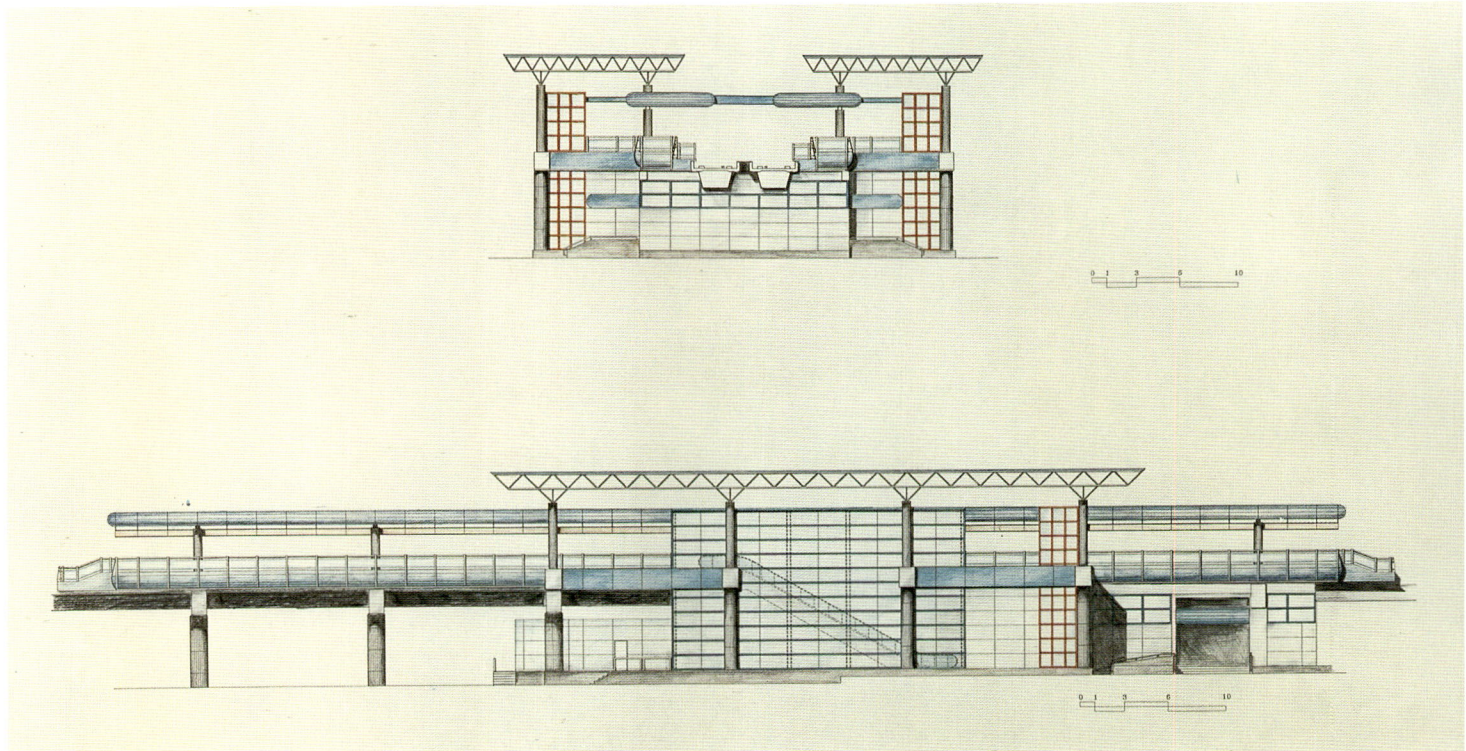

5

Harbor Terminal and Visitor Center, Taichung

Design (Competition) 1994
Taichung, Taiwan
Taichung Harbor Bureau
23,735 square meters

The design criterion for the Harbor
Terminal and Visitor Center in Taichung
is to create a landmark building that can
effectively manage the relationships
amongst different traffic conditions.
Starting from its tower, the terminal
develops along its axis in three-
dimensional space of multiple scales.
The styling of the terminal focuses on the
curved walls to convey a sense of motion
and its relationship to the harbor. Lastly,
the curved lines of the tower complete
the exterior styling of the terminal.

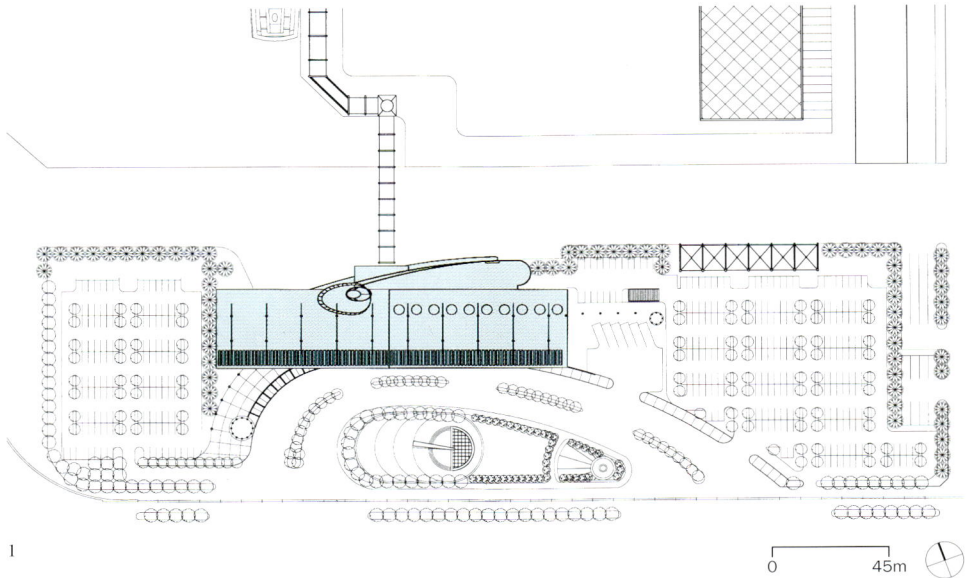

1

0   45m

2

1   Site plan
2   Lobby
3   Aerial
4   Cross section
5   Longitudinal section
6   Perspective

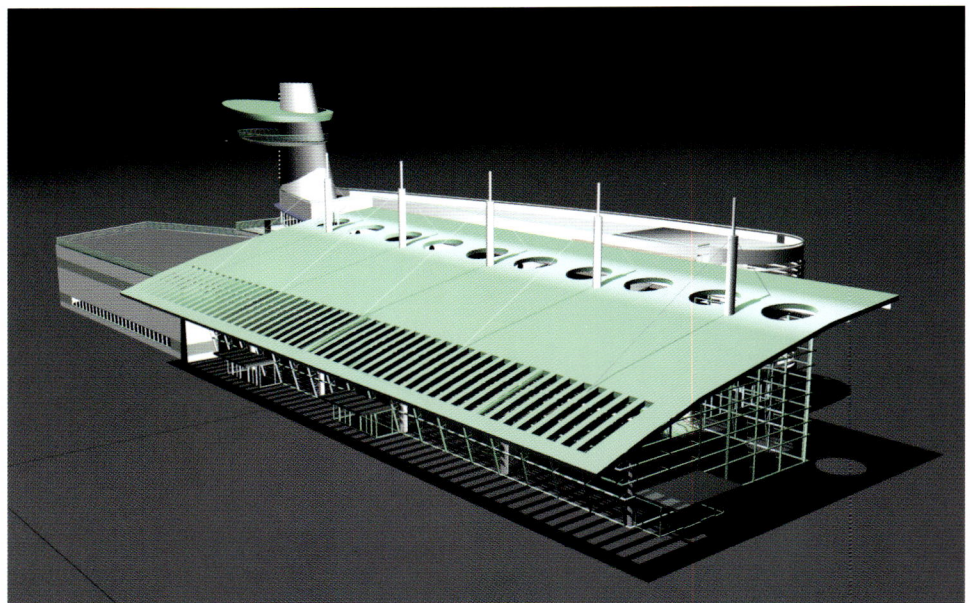

3

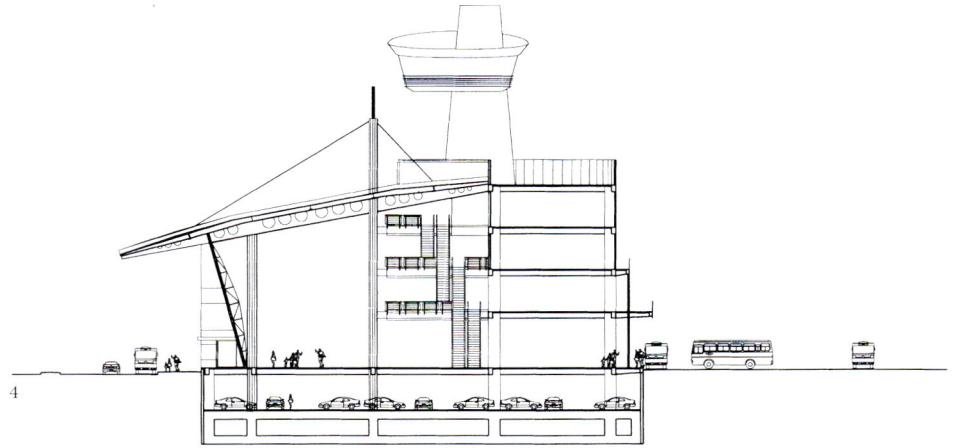

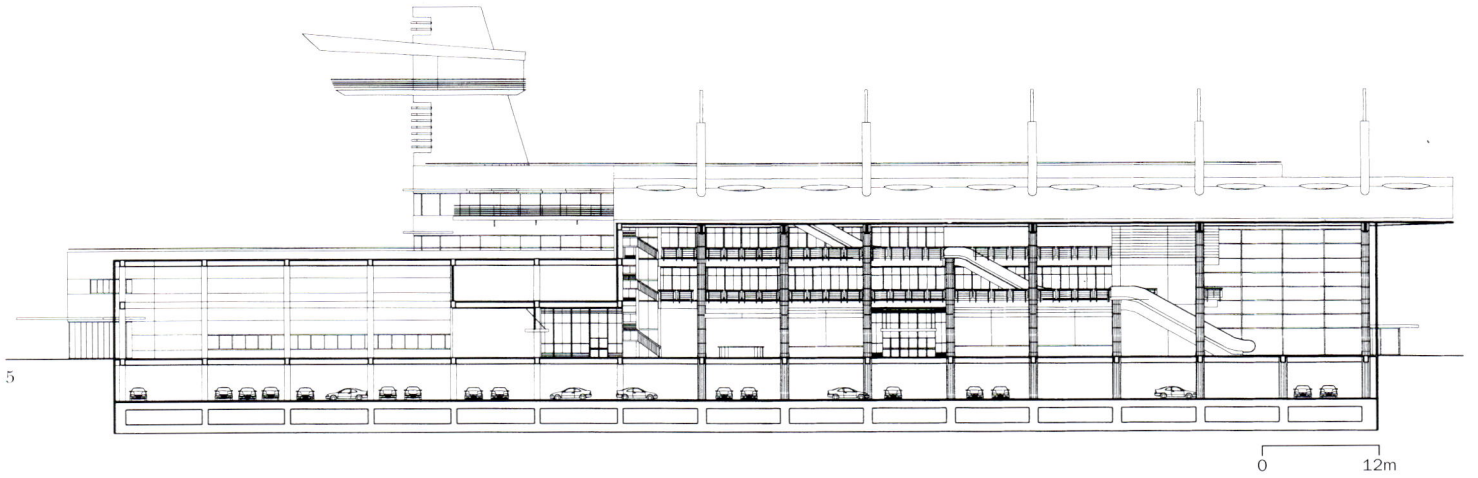

0   12m

4

5

6

Industrial

Sunplus Technology Corporation—Office/Factory Complex

Design/Completion 1995/1996
Hsinchu, Taiwan
Sunplus Technology Corporation
12,909.15 square meters
Precast reinforced concrete panels with steel structure

Sunplus Technology Corporation is located in the Hsinchu science-based industrial park, and the primary goal for our client was to combine functions which had previously been separated on different sites of this science park into a single facility, bringing together manufacturing and office uses. The closer proximity of production facilities, business management, as well as research and development, aims to increase the company's total effectiveness.

For construction, HSP introduced the use of a steel structural frame, as well as precast reinforced concrete panels for the exterior cladding. These techniques reduced construction time by two months, putting the factory into production earlier, and showing the relationship between architectural design and a company's profitability.

On the exterior of this building, a dramatic arched form marks the main entrance, defining a corporate symbol for Sunplus Technology Corporation. Energy conservation was another critical aspect of this project, and the building design saves an appreciable amount by reductions in electrical power consumption.

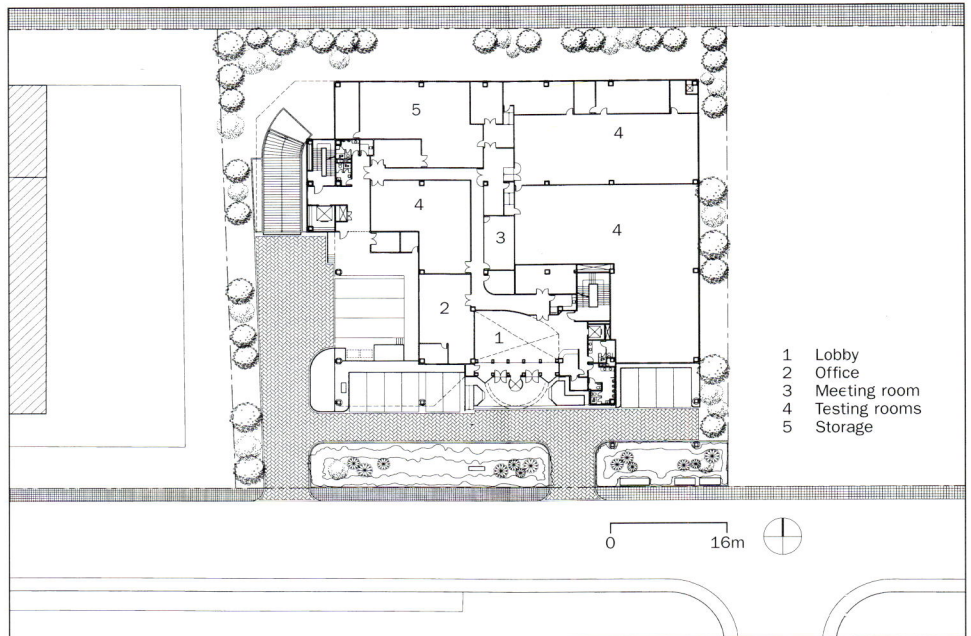

1 Lobby
2 Office
3 Meeting room
4 Testing rooms
5 Storage

1

1 First floor plan
2 Front façade
3 Night view

154

4   Main entrance space frame
5   Lobby

Alpha Telecom Inc., New Facility

Design/Completion 1995/1997
Hsinchu, Taiwan
Alpla Telecom Inc.
16,196.73 square meters
Reinforced concrete
Light and dark blue tile with orange accents

This new facility for Alpha Telecom Inc., in the Hsinchu science-based industrial park, primarily produces components for telecommunications systems. The overall building complex is arranged to accommodate the long, narrow site.

The planning and layout of the interior space were designed to produce open plans and maximum efficiency, while the massing of the building expresses the functional division into a six-story portion for administrative offices and a four-story portion for the manufacturing areas. The exterior is a dynamic composition of light and dark blue tile, with orange accents, designed to express the corporate image of Alpha Telecom.

The interior space planning organizes functional areas around service cores. Thus, the primary circulation for both office areas and factory production areas use efficient horizontal movement. The main entrance lobby is recessed, using a slanted glass wall to draw attention to the entrance and to express the first floor special exhibit area, as well as drawing in natural light and views of the landscape.

1

1   View from the northwest
2   View from the southwest
3   View from the southeast
4   First floor plan
5   View from the south

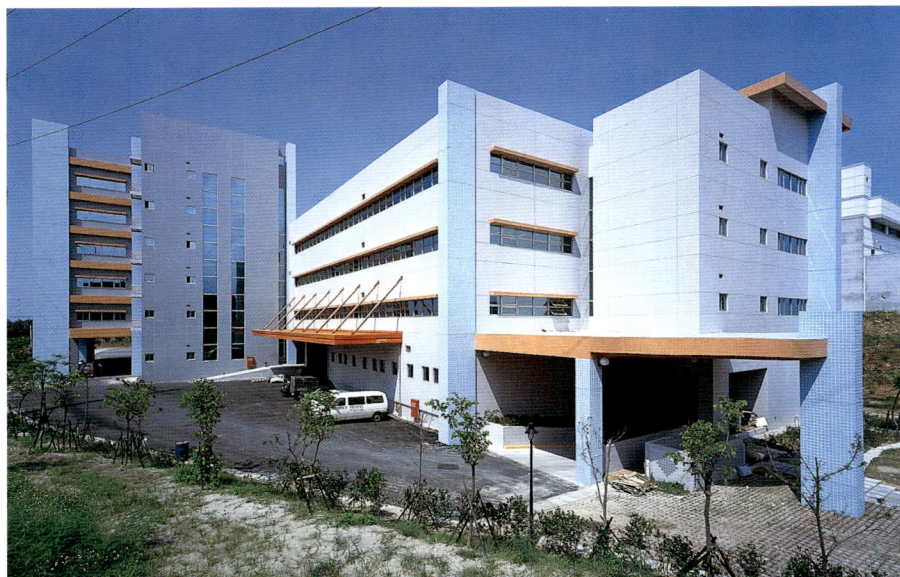

2

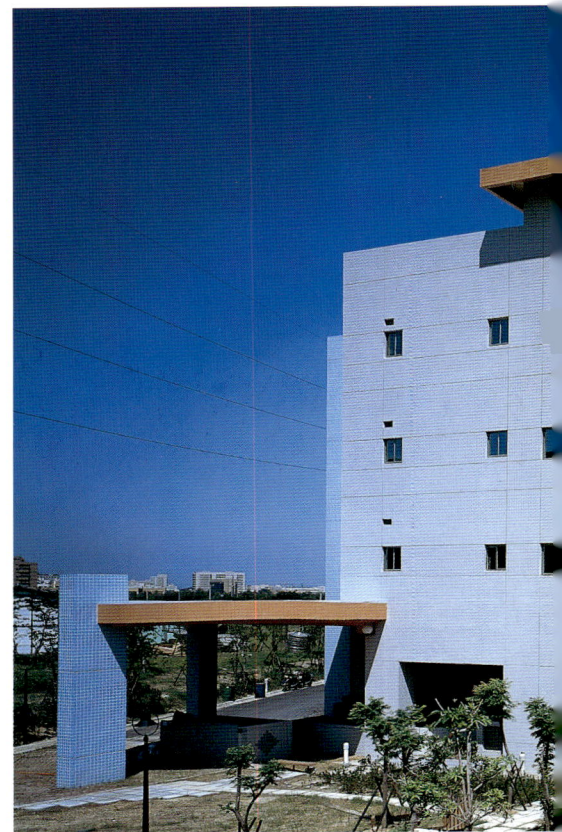

3

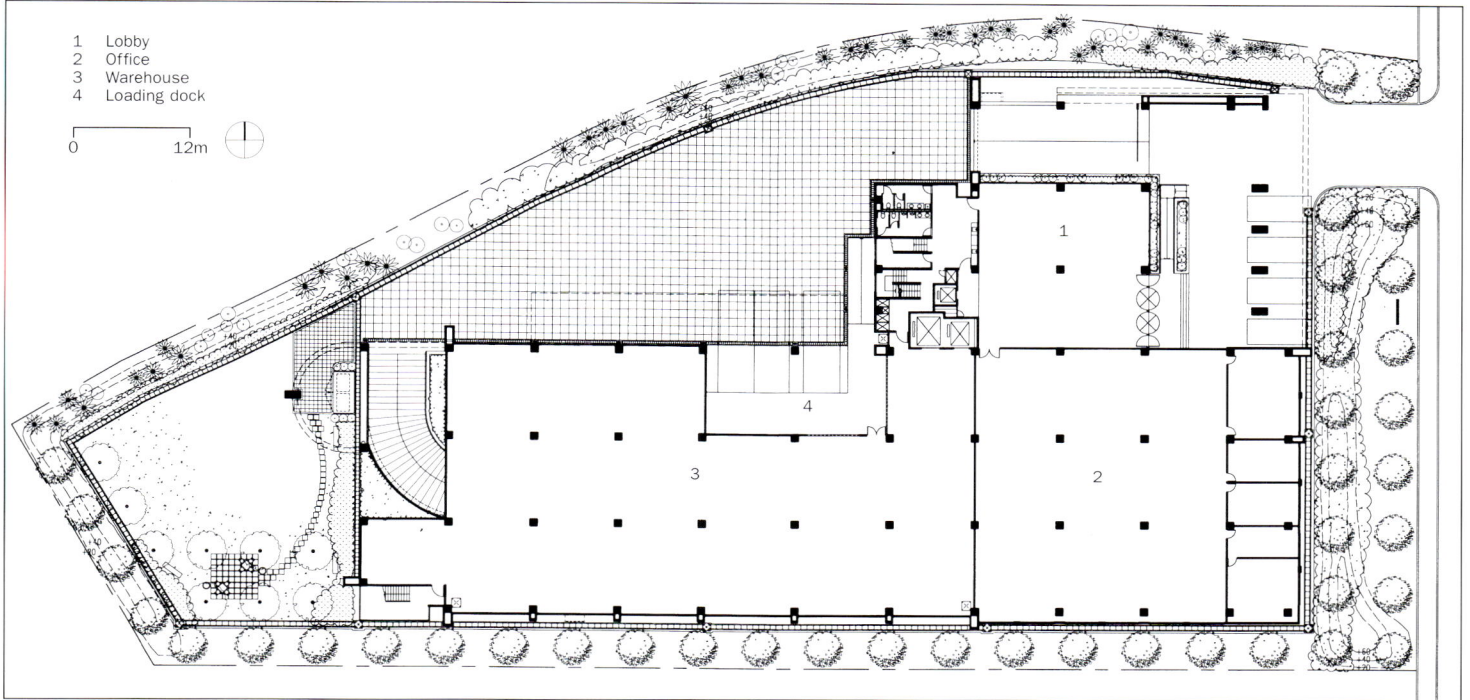

1 Lobby
2 Office
3 Warehouse
4 Loading dock

0   12m

Yageo Corporation Kaohsiung Factory III

Design/Completion 1998/2001
Kaohsiung, Taiwan
Yageo Corporation
21284.35 square meters
Reinforced concrete
Aluminium panel curtainwall

Yageo Corporation is a reputable telecommunications corporation known for its resisters and other electronic parts. In this project, Yageo set out to build a brand new office and manufacturing facility in Kaohsiung county, as part of a goal to increase product type and increase productivity.

Two to four-story reinforced concrete buildings and traditional metal deck factories cover the existing site surroundings. This project aims to re-create Yageo's hi-tech corporate image, making it different from the lifeless and boring "manufacture machine" which could be commonly seen. In its design planning, the aim is to create a factory that is precise, efficient, humanized, modern, and hi-tech:

- Efficient space for manufacturing
- Space organization for ease of management
- Humanized working environment
- Architecturally expresses precise and efficient corporate image.

1

1   View from the east
2   Front façade
3   First floor plan
4   View from the west

2

1 Lobby
2 Storage
3 Factory
4 Loading dock

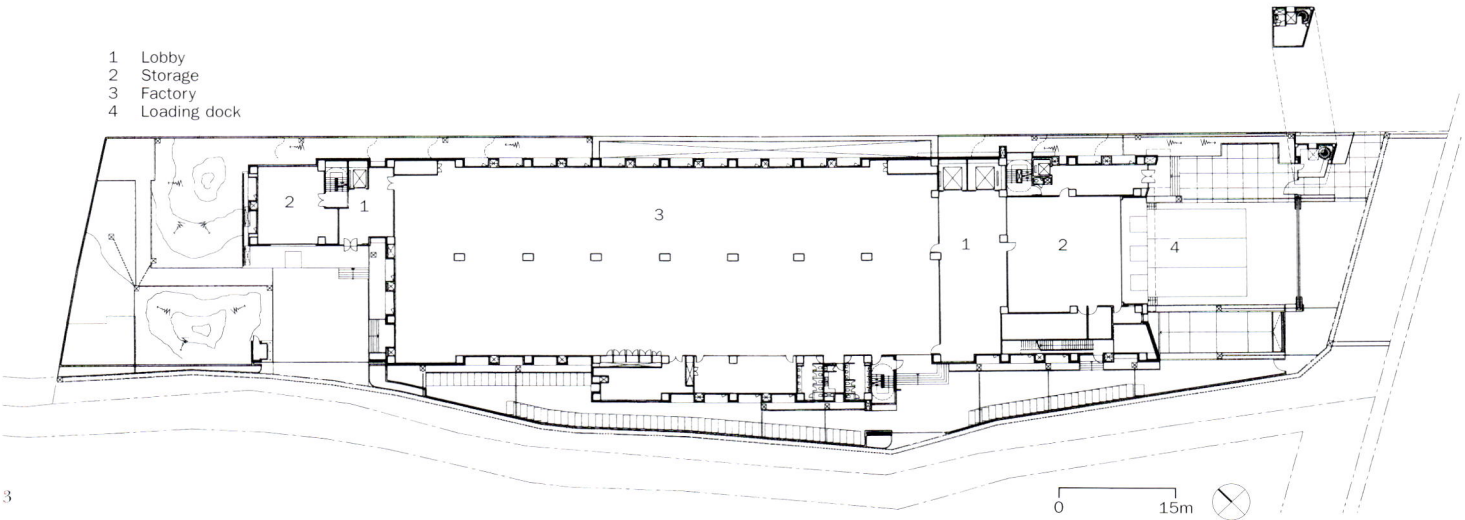

3

0   15m

4

5   Landscape of restaurant
6   Lounge
Following pages:
    Lobby

5

Medical/Research

Institute of Modern History, Academia Sinica

Design/Completion 1989/1993
Taipei, Taiwan
Academia Sinica
5,240.84 square meters
Reinforced concrete

The program which guides the Institute of Modern History, and which formed the basis of this design, is based upon extending the academic tradition of the humanities, as well as developing the spirit of our contemporary times through research.

This building makes a dramatic change from the traditional appearance of the Institute's former quarters, presenting a lively and richly developed exterior, reflecting the research into society and life conducted within. As part of its architectural language, this project uses inset windows with contemporary glazed corners, blending the contemporary and the classical traditions.

The interior spaces of the Institute are organized around a core composed of common spaces, such as meeting rooms and elevators, together with a pair of octagonal stairways. Branching off from this core, the scholars' offices are distributed in two wings that enclose an exterior courtyard. At the turning points and the ends of these two wings there are spaces for informal meetings or relaxation, brightening the corridors and providing views to the outside, and fostering the spirit of cooperative study, which is the goal of this institute.

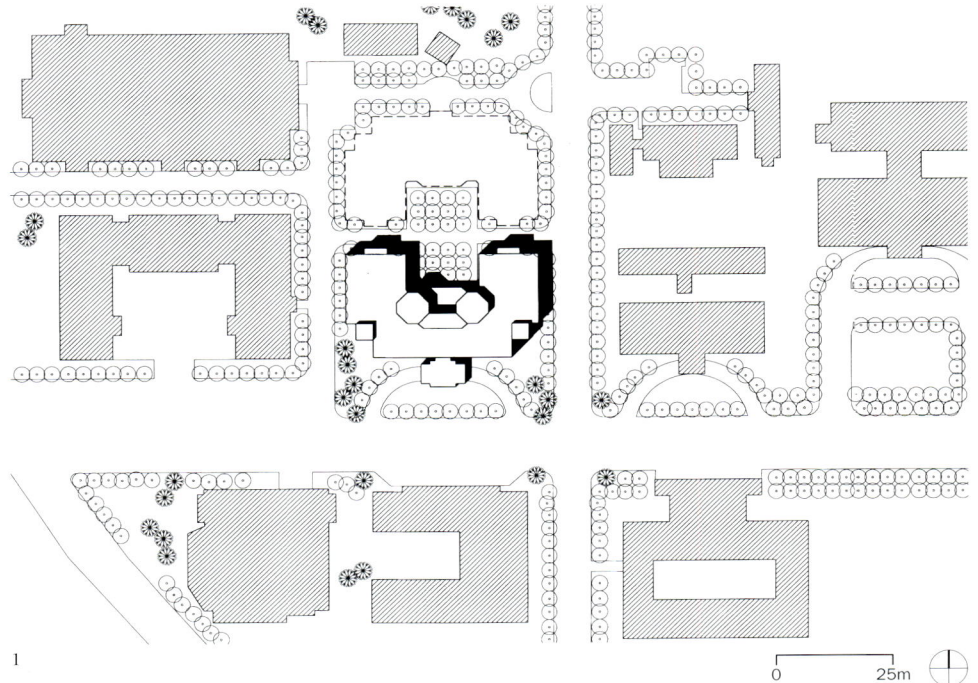

1

0   25m

1   Site plan
2   View from the southeast
3   View from the northeast

2

3

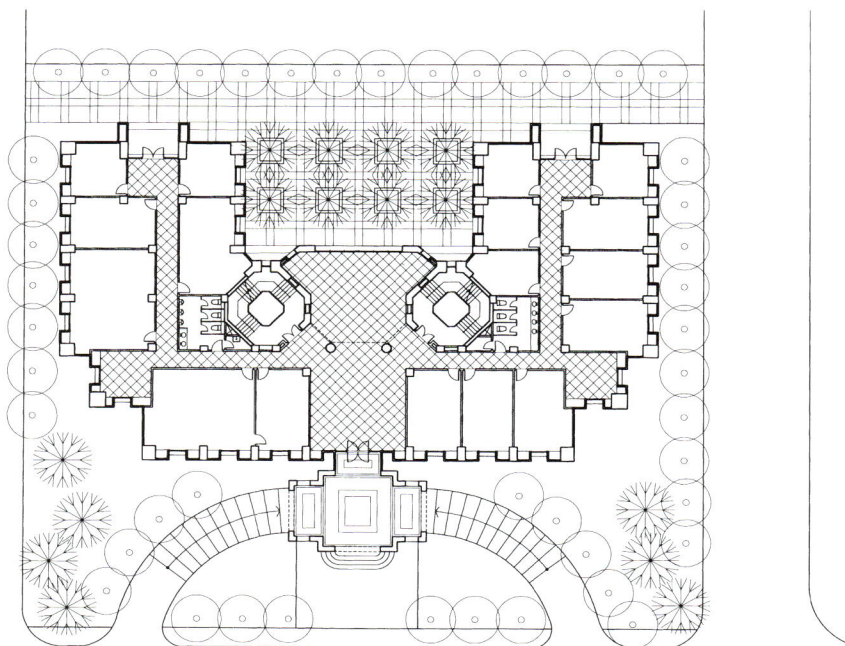

4

0   8m

5

6

7

Institute of Biomedical Sciences, Academia Sinica

Design/Completion 1989/1995
Taipei, Taiwan
Academia Sinica
26,764 square meters
Reinforced concrete structure
Deep window recesses and glazed curtainwalls

This expansion project approximately doubled the size of the original Biological Research Institute, providing laboratories and academic facilities for all departments of medical research.

The winner of a national design competition, this building uses a combination of deep window recesses and glazed curtainwalls to develop an architectural vocabulary that is both strong and appropriate to this facility. On the interior, in order to humanize the work environment, numerous spaces for relaxation and interaction are used to connect the main research areas. In addition, numerous sunscreens are incorporated on the east and west elevations, reducing the size of air conditioning units required, as well as the operating expense.

1   Partial façade
2   First floor plan
3   Original building

1

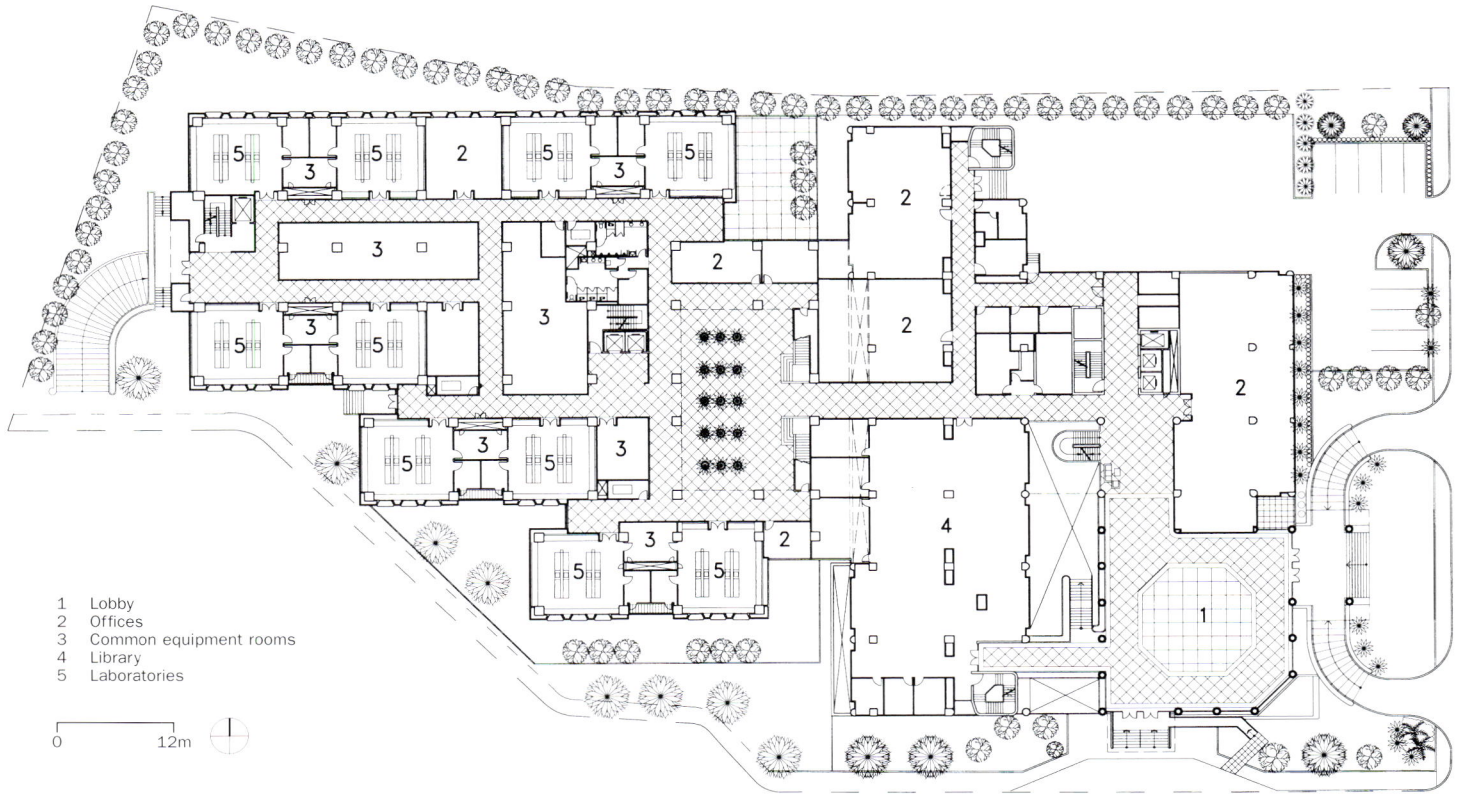

2

1 Lobby
2 Offices
3 Common equipment rooms
4 Library
5 Laboratories

0   12m

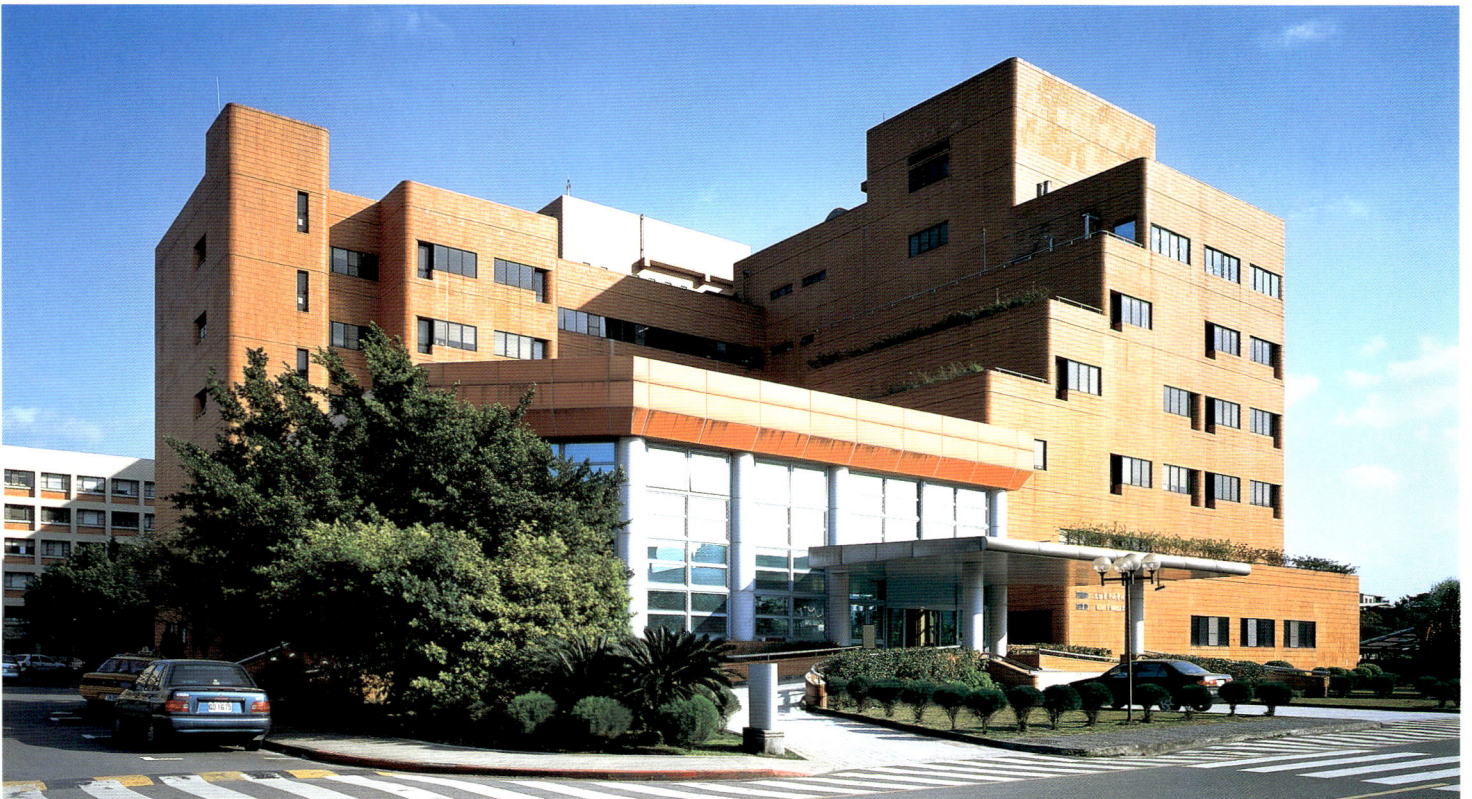

3

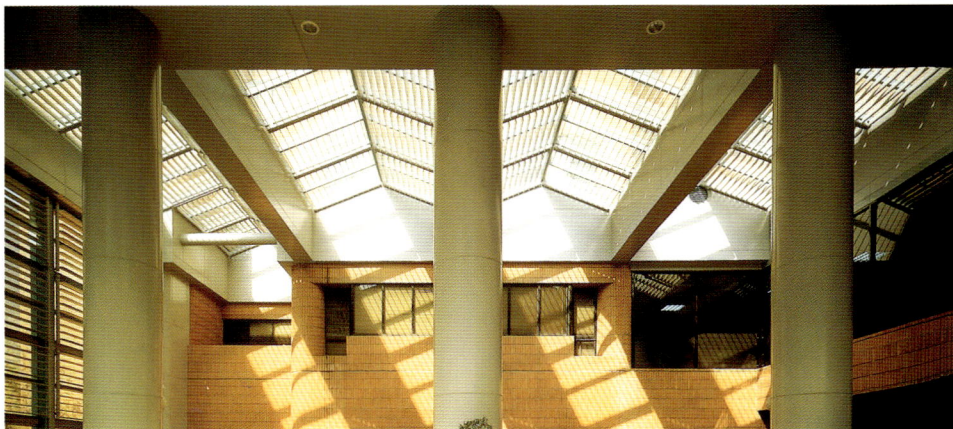

4　View from the south
5　Lobby's skylight
6　Original building's lobby

Cancer Center, Koo Foundation

Design/Completion 1992/1997
Taipei, Taiwan
Koo Foundation
Joint-venture firm: NBBJ Architects Associates
63,240 square meters
Reinforced concrete
White ceramic tiles and horizontal fenestration

Planned and designed in collaboration with the American architectural consulting firm NBBJ, this facility has an outpatient capacity of 1,200 people per day, 350 beds and nine operating rooms. The institution aims to raise national standards for treatment and care of cancer patients, as well as to train the finest in medical staff. The building's massing makes effective use of an irregular site spanning between two major roads, and reduces the impact of neighboring industrial usage. The site layout also provides a maximum of landscaped green space, beyond that required by code.

The building itself is arranged to accommodate an institution for blood donation and research, which has differing requirements from the rest of the hospital. These two different uses appear separate above grade, although they are connected by two basement levels containing common services and parking. A skylight atrium entrance brings natural light to the underground levels. The patient rooms are grouped in three clusters, each in an angled arrangement, with the nurses' station and service rooms at the center enabling nursing staff to have more efficient surveillance of the patient rooms on two sides.

1   View from the south
2   First and second floor plans
3   Main entrance

1

176

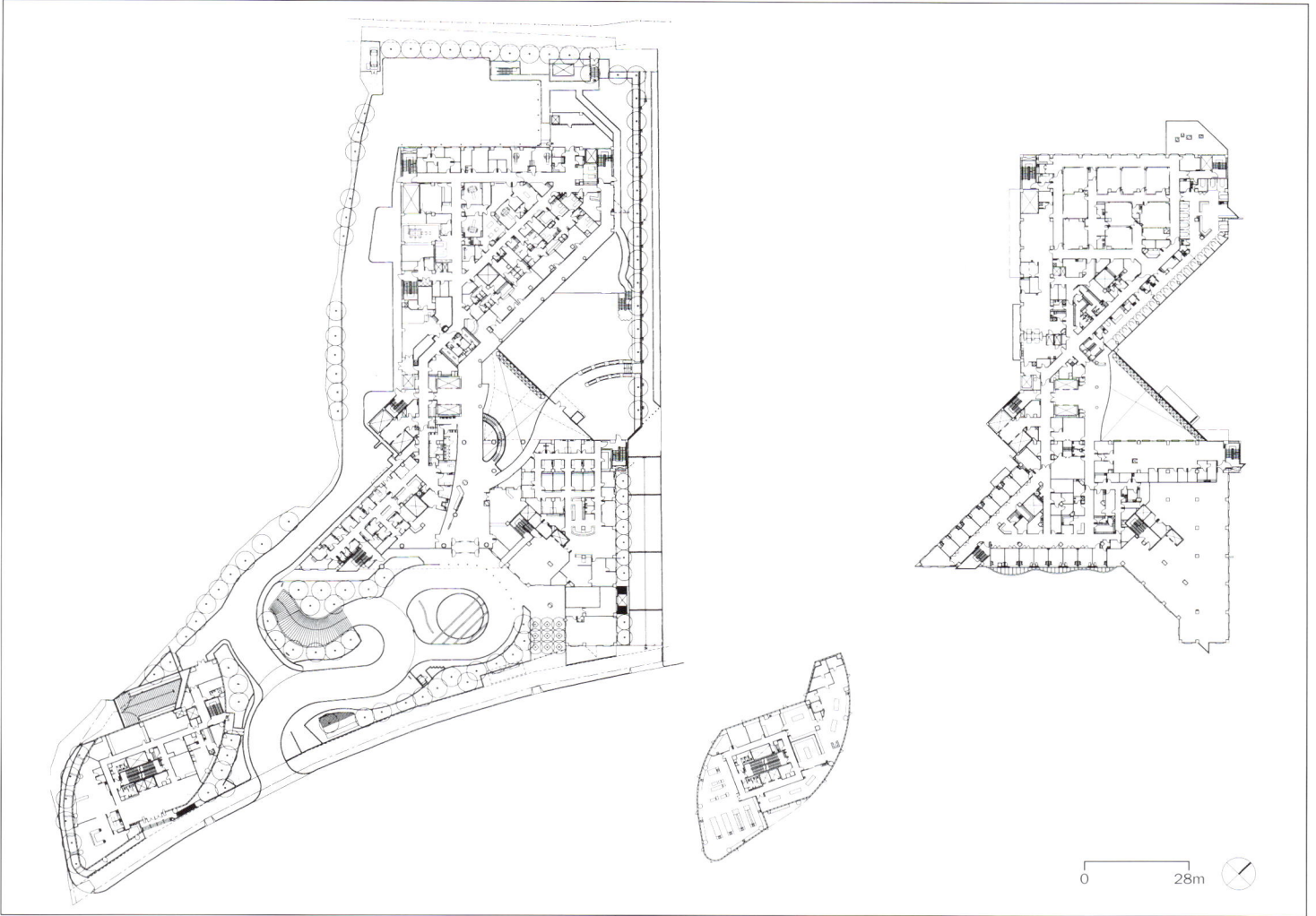

2

3

4

5

6

4   View of the central courtyard
5   Main lobby
6&7   Overview from the third floor looking at the atrium
Following pages:
    Grand stair of the atrium

7

Housing/Religious

Good Shepherd Church

Design/Completion 1965/1967
Taipei, Taiwan
Taiwan Episcopal Church
2,500 square meters
Masonry wall construction
Red brick wall finish

The Good Shepherd Church was completed in 1967. The Church was designed to be a low-profile building, making a strong attempt to merge religious architecture with the surrounding buildings. It also attempts to combine the essence of Christian architecture and the religious architecture of the East.

Its site plan mimics that of the Confucius Temple. It is symmetrically organized, with two wings and a central courtyard. Upon entering the central courtyard, the main hall is located on the central axis. With the office spaces and Sunday school classrooms located on either wing, the main hall is more imposing. The double pitch roof, red brick wall finish, and its arcade accentuate the comfort and beauty true to traditional Chinese architecture. Its horizontal form provides a friendly atmosphere which differs from the verticality of churches in the West. The Good Shepherd Church plays an important role in the morphosis of the local religious architecture.

1   Church entrance

1

Chapel, St. John's & St. Mary's Institute of Technology

Design/Completion 1967/1968
Tamsui, Taiwan
St John's & St Mary's Institute of Technology
1,200 square meters
Reinforced concrete structure

The Chapel of St. John's & St. Mary's Institute of Technology is situated left of the main entrance, creating a visual focal point at entry to the campus. Its elegant and simple exterior, along with its high roof, conveys a sense of enlightenment so natural to a religious building. Viewed from any angle, its symmetrically cross-shaped layout presents a constant visual image. Much like a sculpture, its contours create effects of light and shadow that is eyecatching.

The rectangular-shaped area for Mass serves as a nucleus. Its altar is centrally situated directly beneath the highest point of the ceiling and is surrounded by benches for 300 people. Other spaces are arranged in a radial and symmetrical fashion, including foyer, locker room, rest rooms etc. These spaces of lower ceiling height break away from the central high roof that adds to the richness of its volume and the effects of light and shadow.

1   View of the chapel

1

College Chapel, Tamsui Aletheia University

Design/Completion 1993/1997
Taipei, Taiwan
Tamsui Oxford University
6206.54 square meters
Reinforced concrete structure
Grey tiles, granite and red brick facing

The site for this project has an exceptionally rich historical context, with a 16th-century Dutch fort to the west, the Oxford Academy—dating from the 19th century—on the north, and another historic brick structure to the east. Thus, the design of this project required the development of a historical style to complement the surrounding buildings so that they formed a unified ensemble.

The development of the architectural style was done in accordance with an expression of Christian beliefs, using a form vocabulary of pointed arches modeled on the image of hands folded in prayer, and a roof form expressing the Trinity. These forms are used for window and door openings throughout the building, so that there is a complete and unified aesthetic sensibility that can be viewed from every direction.

Since this project is in the subtropical climate of Taiwan, a partially enclosed arcade is provided around the building to protect the interior from direct sunlight, whilst admitting generous amounts of natural light. In addition, this arcade forms a walkway which allows views of the Tamsui River and Mount Kuanyin.

The exterior of this building blends the roof form and the pointed arches with a covering of grey tiles, setting off the other exterior materials of exposed stone aggregate, granite and red brick facing. The form of the building steps down the slope of the hill to minimize its impact on the surrounding buildings, creating a new structure that harmonizes and with its surroundings.

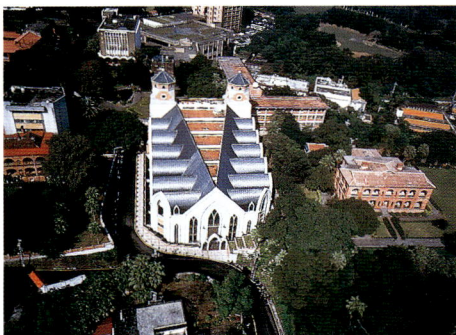

2

0   12m

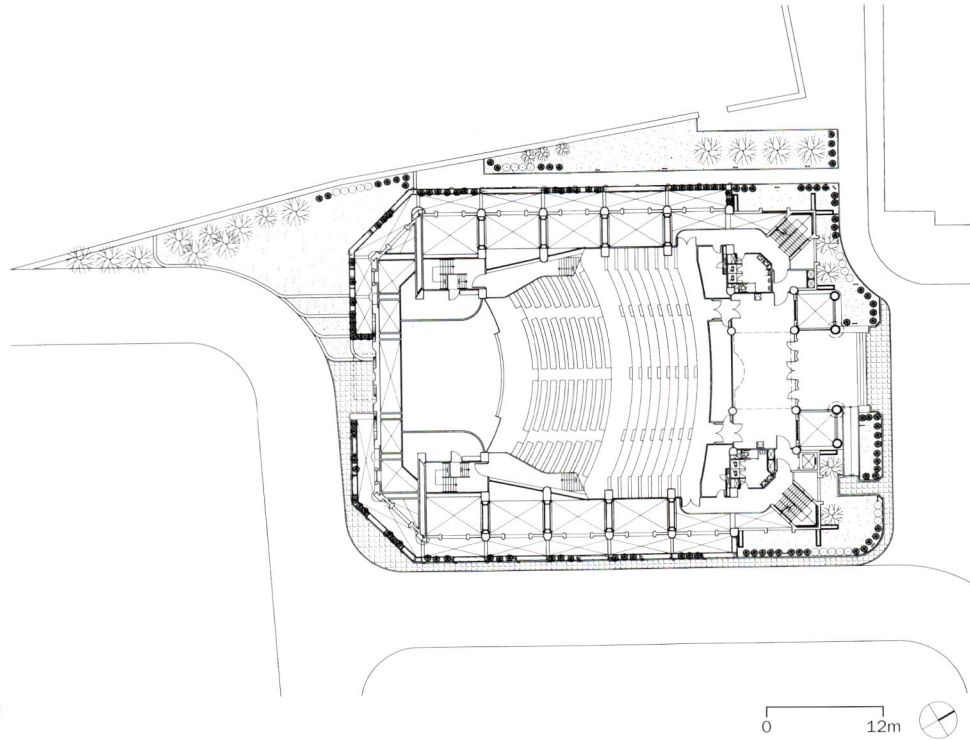

1

3

4

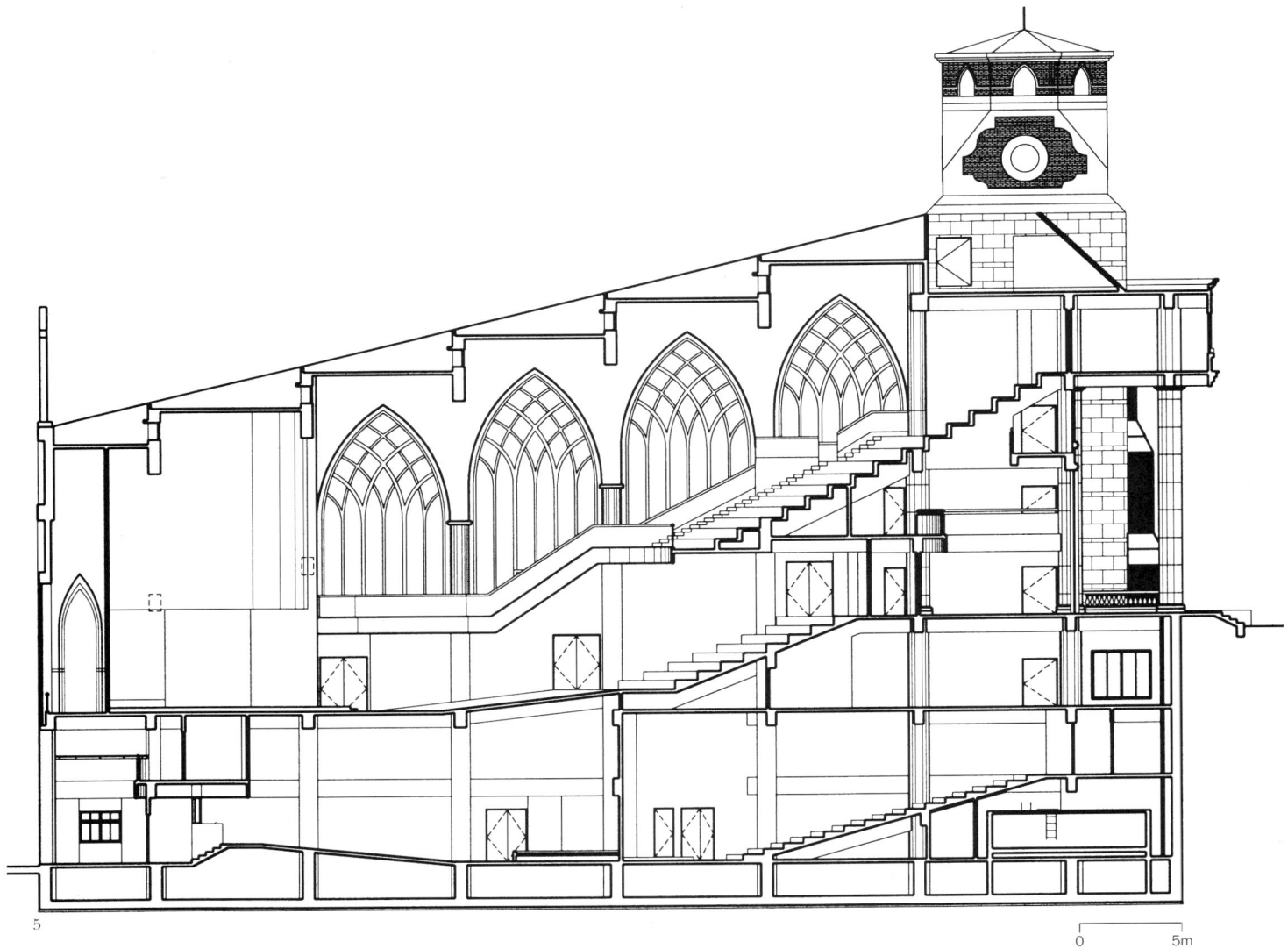

5 Longitudinal section
6 View from the south along the slope of the hill

6

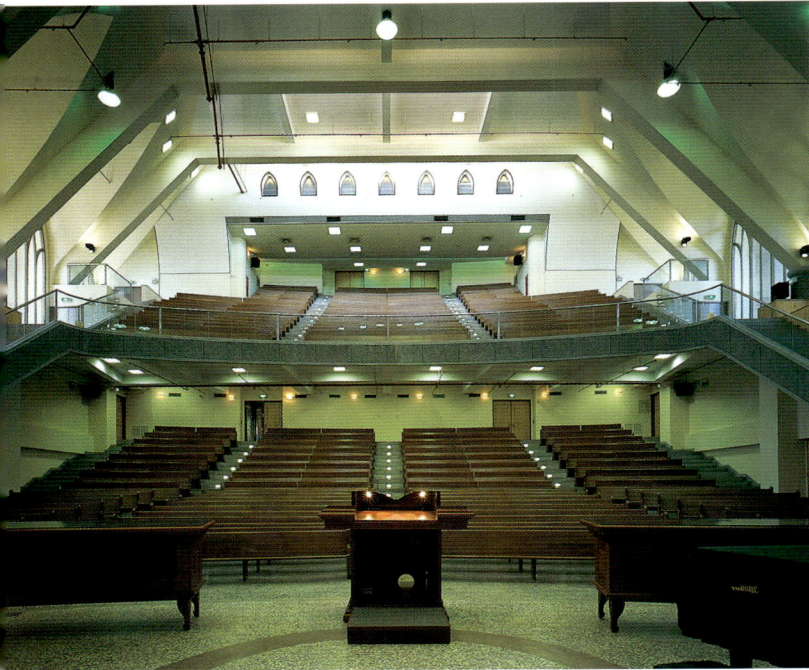

7

8

Cheng-Kung Village Community, Taipei

Design/Completion 1980/1984
Taipei, Taiwan
Taipei City Government
252,936 square meters
Reinforced concrete

City Block Overall Planning

The site remains as one complete block. Within the block, several towers of various heights arise to form groups of apartments linked by walkways and open public squares. The variation in height adds interest to the community. Access roads are placed around the block, while pedestrian walkways branch within the block to form a complete community.

Pedestrian and Car Separation

The community primarily focuses on the pedestrian movements and walkways, and leaves the car entrance paths and readily available parking spaces as secondary focus. As a design criterion, car paths are linked easily to the surrounding community for ease of access, while pedestrian walkways stay close to the homes to provide a quiet and serene living environment.

Parks, Squares, and Axial Systems

There are parks and children's playing areas within the block to provide enough open space. Large open squares have also been provided to allow various types of activities and to encourage interaction amongst residents.

The main axis of pedestrian walkways lie east and west, linking commercial and service facilities. The remaining walkways link the active and quiet zones of the community in a circular fashion.

Public Facilities

Public facilities considered to be necessities for the residents, such as commercial facilities (commercial square, supermarket, retail stores), service facilities (daycare center, kindergarten, post office, bank, police station), residents' facilities (residents' activity center, management office), and public facilities (electrical power, water supply, telecommunications, gas etc.) have all been provided for to ensure the quality of the residents' living environment.

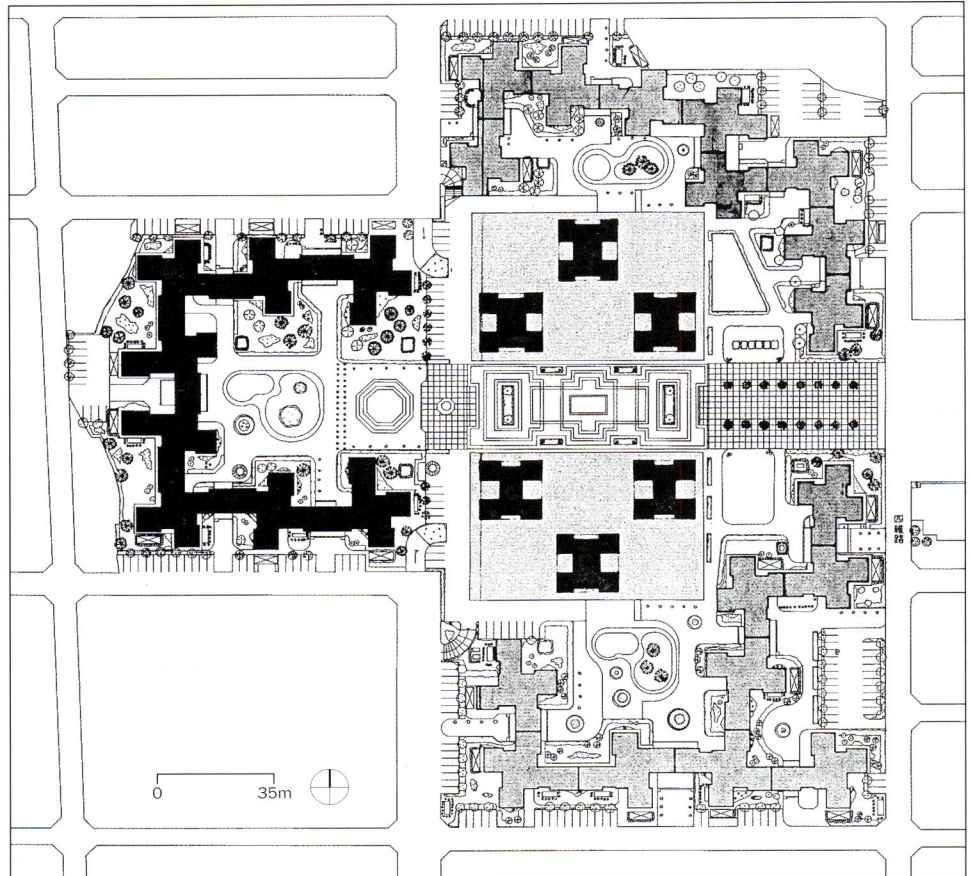

1

2

3

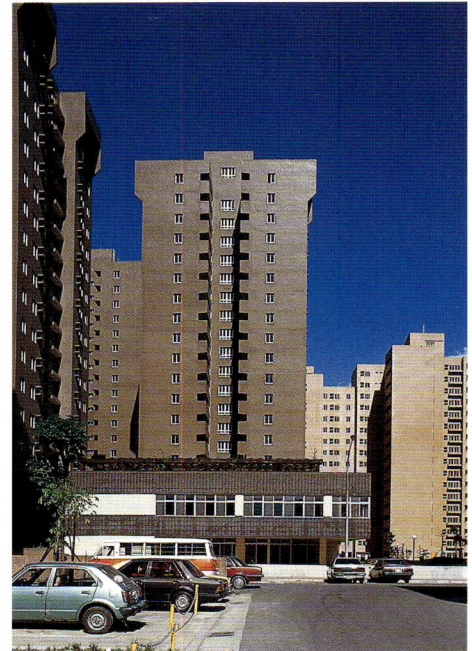

4

1   Site plan
2   Linked walkways
3   Semi-exterior public space
4   View from the southwest
5   Apartment building

Green Village

Design/Completion 1997/2001
Taipei, Taiwan
Continental Engineering Corporation
30,695 square meters
Reinforced concrete structure
Roof tiles complement the walls of stucco and natural stone

This site, in the Taipei suburb of Hsin Tien, is surrounded on three sides by the rolling hills of An Keng and looks out from the fourth side to the distant skyline of Taipei. The main object of this project's design has been to preserve the natural qualities of the location, where one can still hear birdcalls and see sunrises over the mountains.

This project, which is the second district of the first phase of a larger residential development, was planned and designed separately by our office. In order to distinguish itself from earlier residential developments, the project takes its design inspiration from the Spanish-style houses of southern California, USA. Here, sloped roofs of blue-grey roof tiles complement the walls of stucco and natural stone, expressing a harmony with nature, and the idea of respecting the Earth. The colors are clean and simple, providing an architectural vision different from the ostentatious display seen elsewhere, creating an environment of mellow stability and calm—an architectural environment that shows an alternative to the routine style of surrounding developments.

1

1   Site plan
2   Type A first floor plan
3   Type A second floor plan
4   Type A third floor plan
5   Type A elevation rendering
Following pages:
    Type B elevation rendering

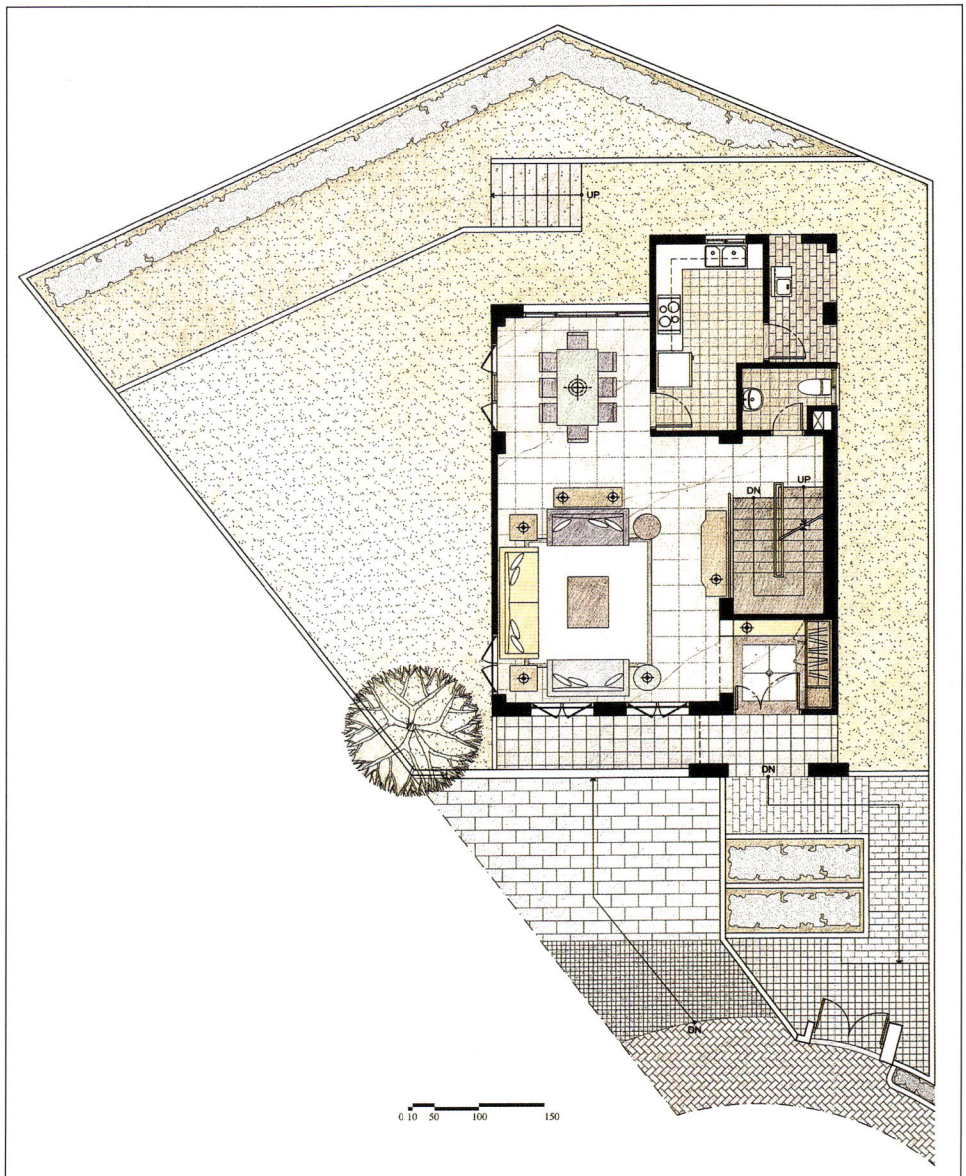

2

196

3   4

5

七0年末四也

100坪情形

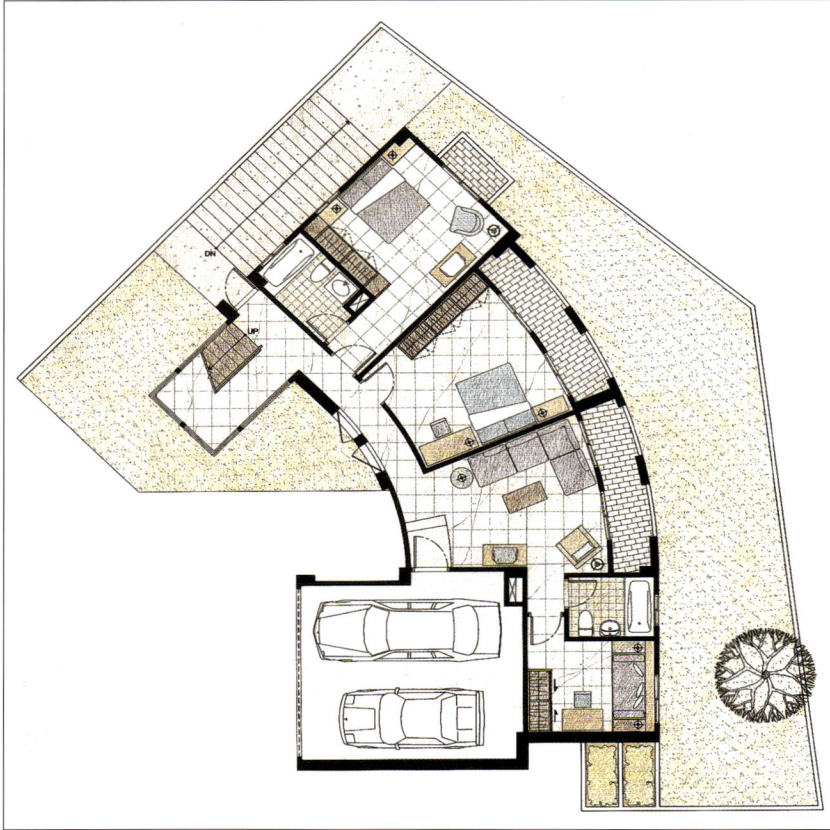

7

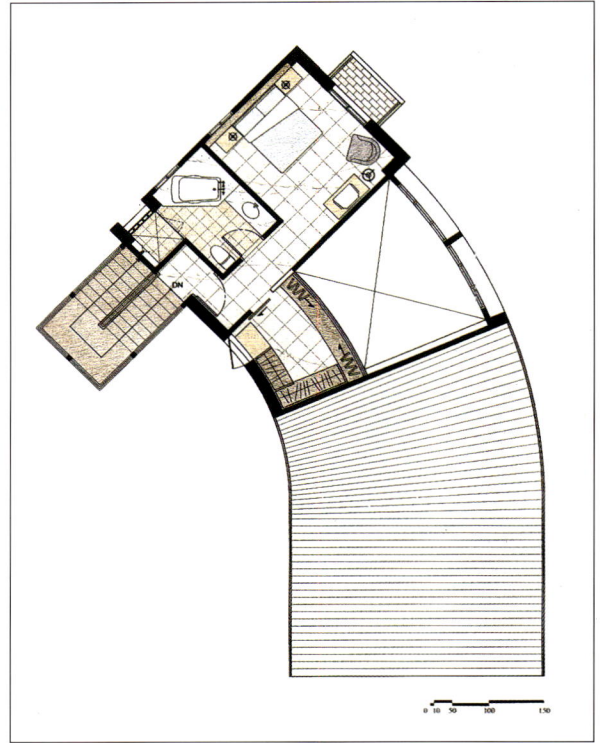

8

7   Type B first floor plan
8   Type B third floor plan
9–12   Building type study model

9

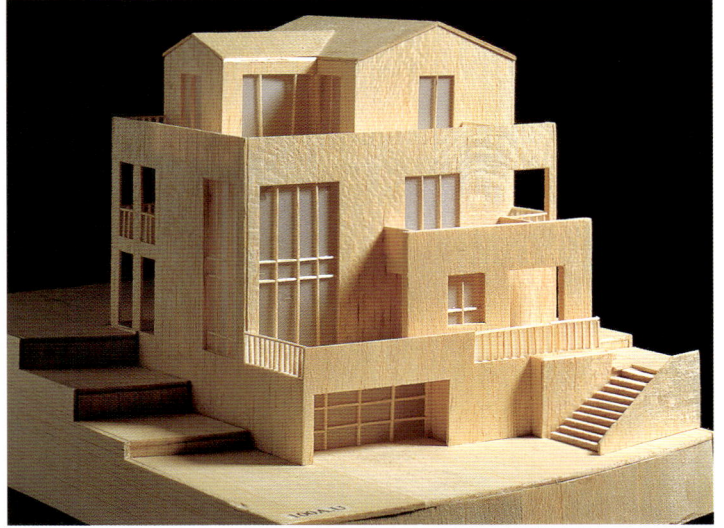

10

11

12

Ray Chang Tower

Design/Completion 1998/2004
Taipei, Taiwan
Ray Chang Development Co. Ltd
37,000 square meters
Curtainwall and recessed terrace with steel-reinforced concrete structure
Joint-venture firm: Pei Cobb Freed & Partners, USA

Planned and designed in collaboration with the American architectural consulting firm of PCF & P, this building will be a 126-meter landmark on Jen-Ai Circle.

It is located at the east–southeast corner of Jen-Ai Circle. The site faces the circle in a length of 45 meters. The project will be comprised of two parts: first floor to the seventh floor will be a bank headquarters, eighth floor to the 34th floor will be luxury apartments. Facing Jen-Ai Circle and Jen-Ai Road will be a landscape designed to give a special visual effect.

The mass of the high-rise building, accentuated by its curtainwall, recessed terrace, and specially designed structural members, will provide a stunning image.

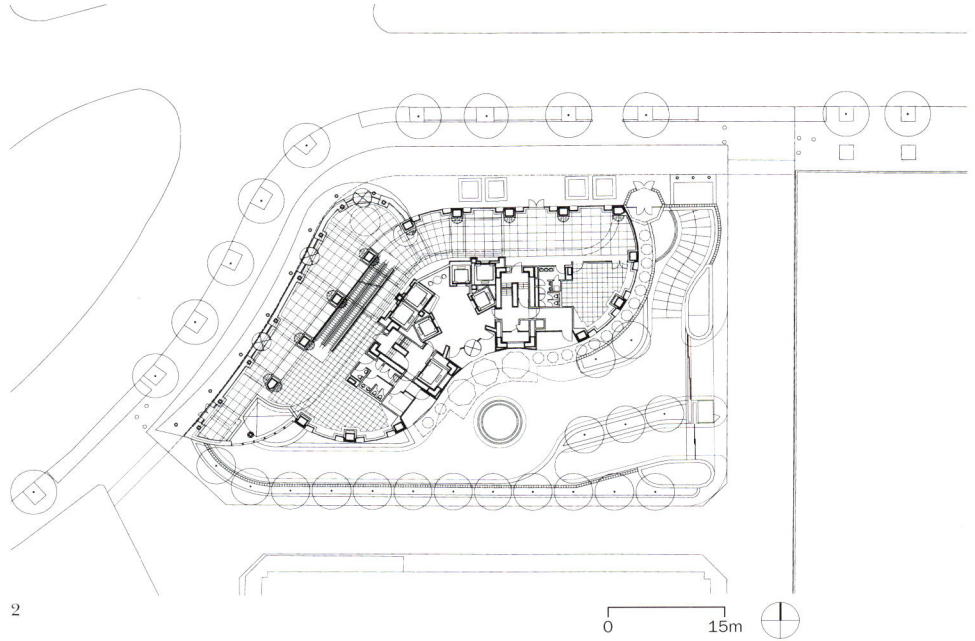

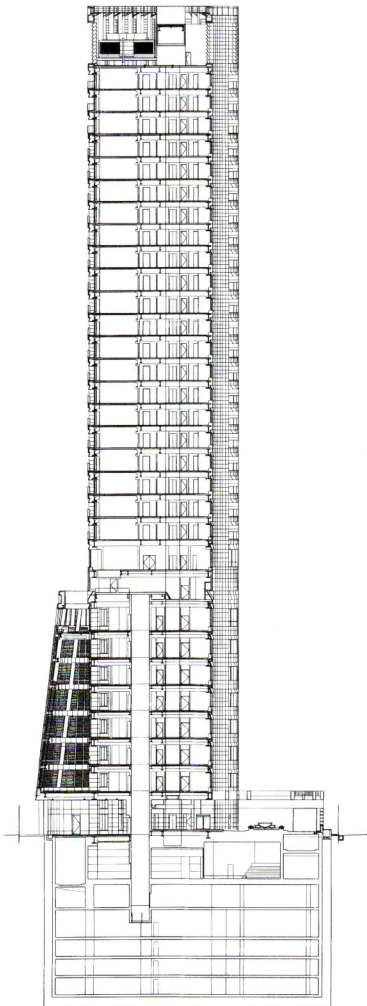

2

0   15m

1

3

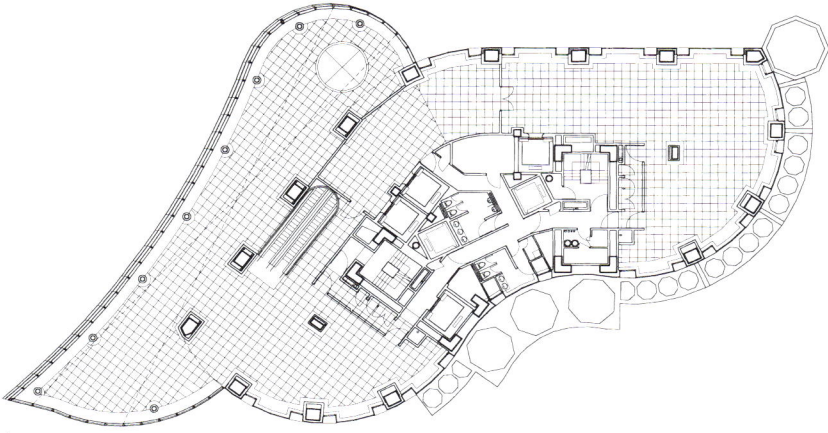

4

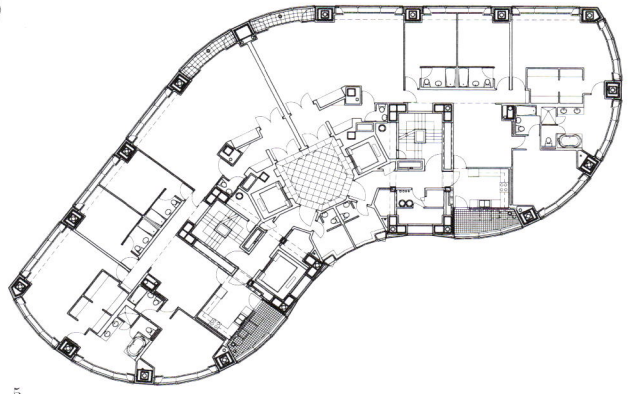

5

6

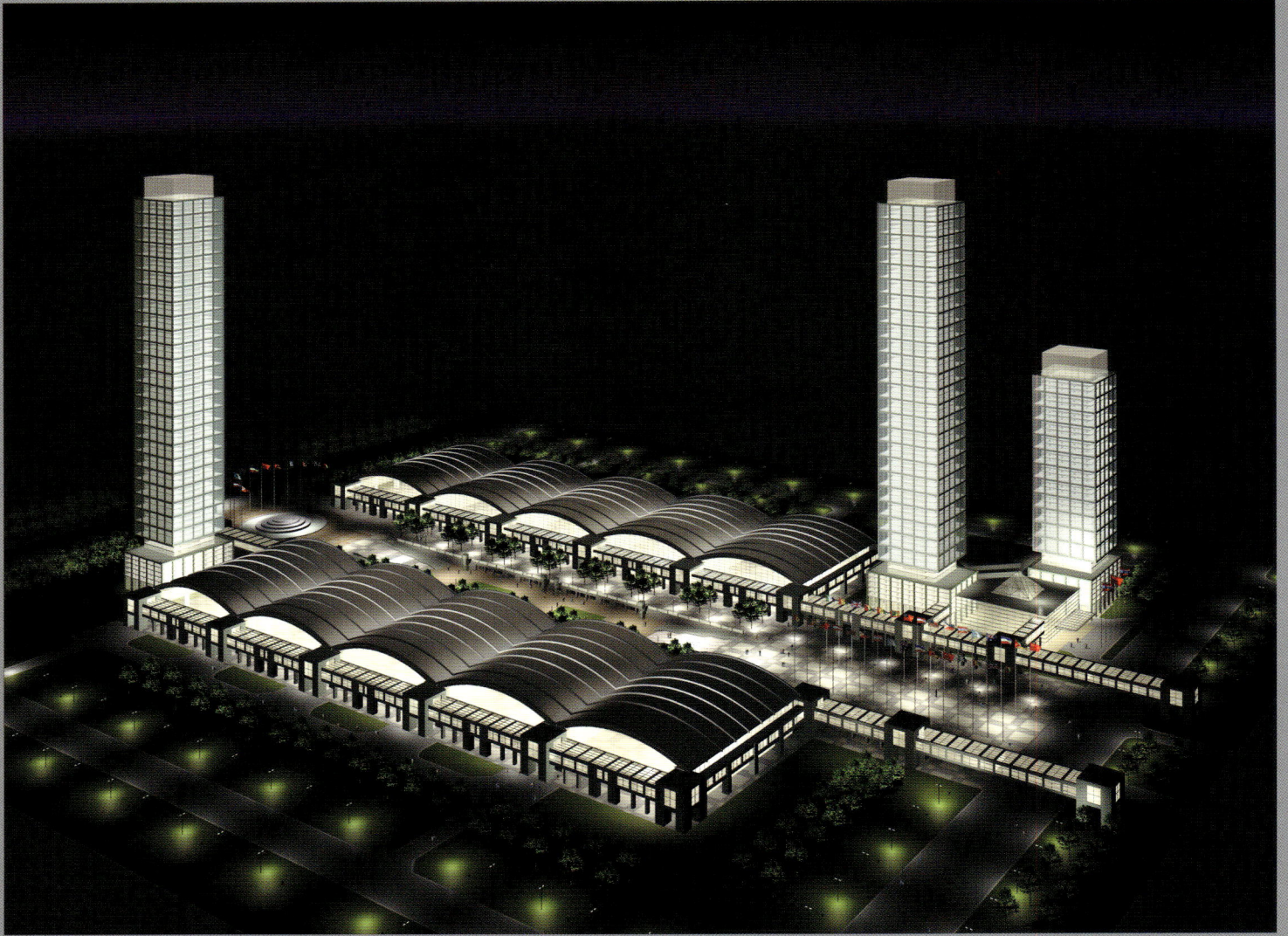

Planning

Campus Planning, National Chung-Cheng University

Planning/Completion 1988/1989
Chiayi, Taiwan
National Chung-Cheng University
131.59 hectares

National Chung-Cheng University is situated in Minhsiung, Chiayi county in the southern part of Taiwan. It is a major university built on what was once a vast sugar plantation. The planning and design principles are as follows.

An Open University—the idea that activities of a university campus should overlap and be integrated with the surrounding environment. This concept is reflected in the arrangements of the campus entrances and the location of dormitory areas adjacent to existing neighborhood services.

Structure for Growth

An organization that will accommodate current functional requirements, as well as provide for continued future growth of individual colleges. Accordingly, an essentially concentric organization where growth is organized outward from a nucleus, with each group of academic facilities tied together by a large-scale circulation pattern, is developed.

Use of Natural Landforms

Appropriate use of natural landforms, with the central core having a natural axis determined by two parallel valleys. Therefore, the central area was retained as a landscaped mall, and the natural watercourses were dammed to create lakes, forming a natural definition for the academic area, and clarifying the sense of orientation within campus.

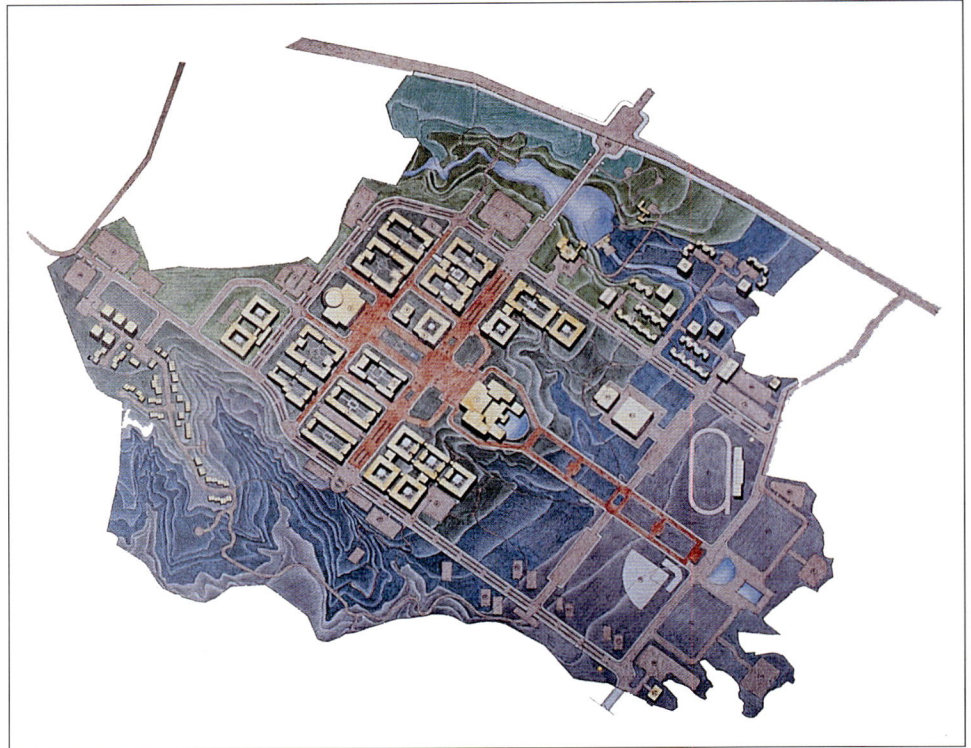

1

1   Campus site plan
2   Distant view of campus
3   View of the campus main axis

2

3

Taipei Terminal Special District Urban Design and Planning

Planning/Completion 1989/1990
Taipei, Taiwan
Taipei City Government
46.17 hectares
Joint-venture firm: Sasaki, USA
Urban planning, urban design, transportation, architecture, landscape design

The overall objective of the Taipei Terminal Special District Urban Design and Planning Project is to turn the Taipei Main Station into a high-quality, mixed-use district, and to stimulate the redevelopment of the West Gate area and its neighboring districts.

The guiding principles of this project include:

1 Strengthen and enhance the area to become the transportation center of the Taipei metropolis.

2 Stimulate the development of neighboring areas.

3 Provide various open space areas.

4 Strengthen the international city and gateway image.

5 Improve the environmental quality of the metropolis.

6 Upon financial feasibility, join public and private sectors to set up special development organization.

The terminal area will bring in offices, retailers, department stores, and hotels. Major constructions within the area include the Taipei Main Station, underground tunnels, MRT station, Taiwan Motor Transport Main Station, MRT Control Center, an underground parking lot, underground shopping arcade, the East-West Expressway etc. Since this project is located as the gateway to Taipei, the Taipei Main Station building was used as a landmark and several continuous open space systems were planned to highlight the visual axis from the building to the Tamshuei River. At the same time, the building was used to clearly mark the open space areas. Historical construction such as the North Gate, the old Railroad Office, and the Sun Yat-Sen Memorial Park were all included in the consideration.

1

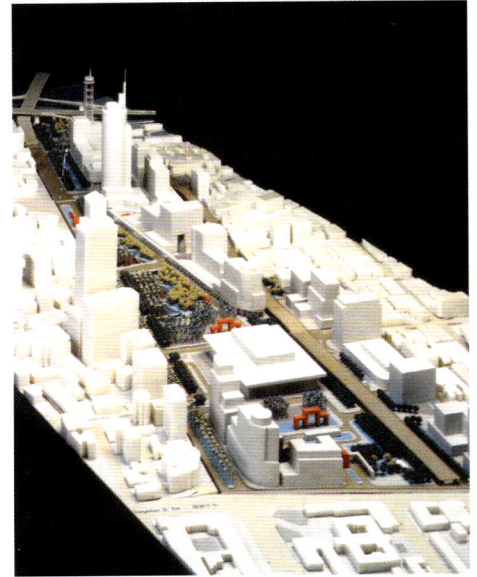
2

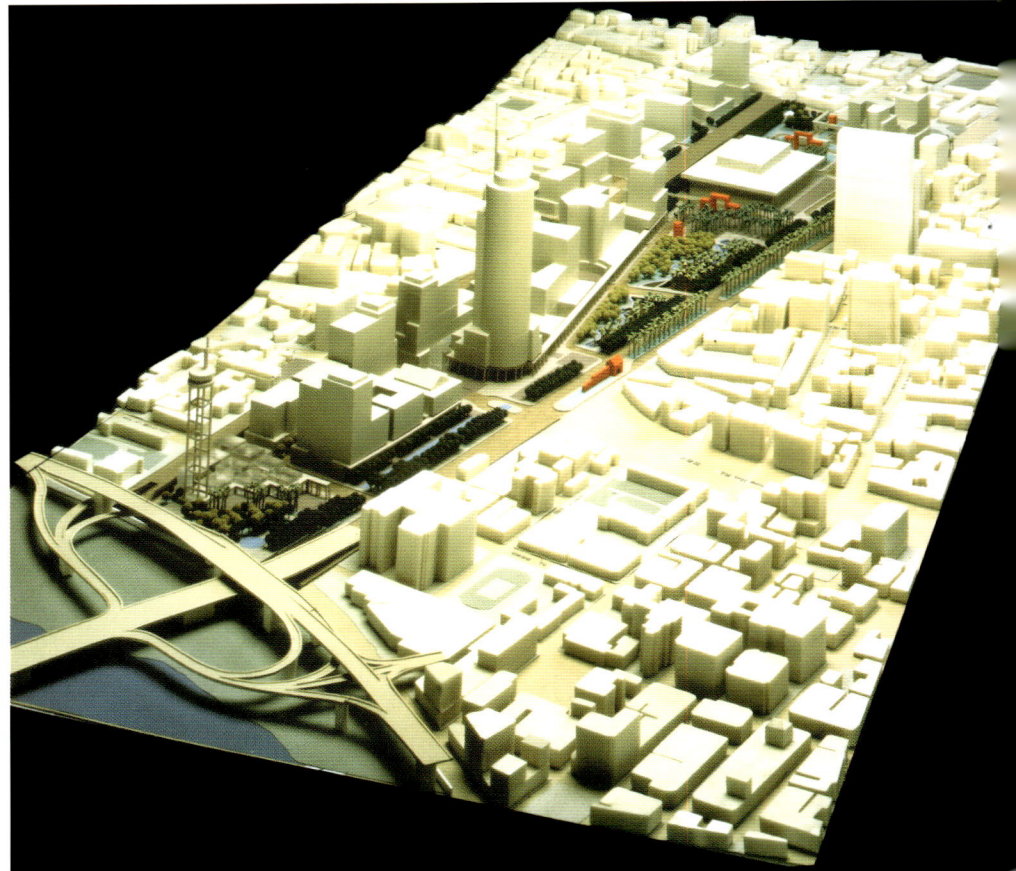
3

1   View from Taipei Main Station
2   Ecological park
3   Site model, view from the river
4   Site plan
5   Central garden

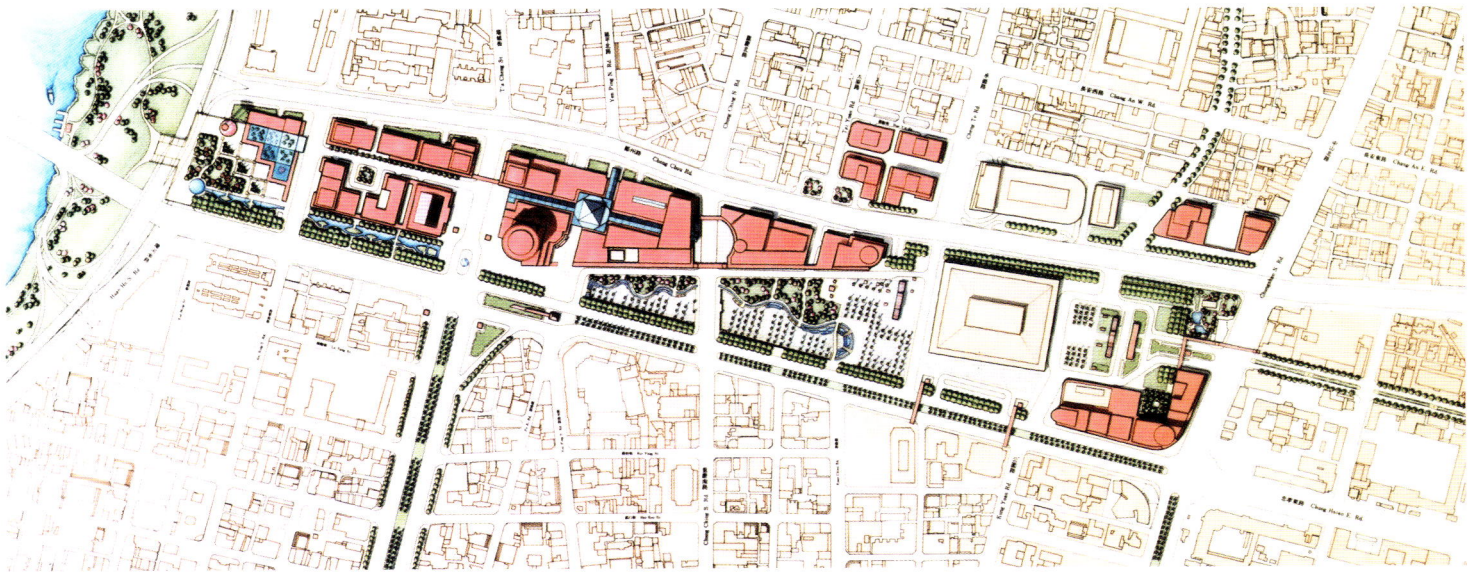

4

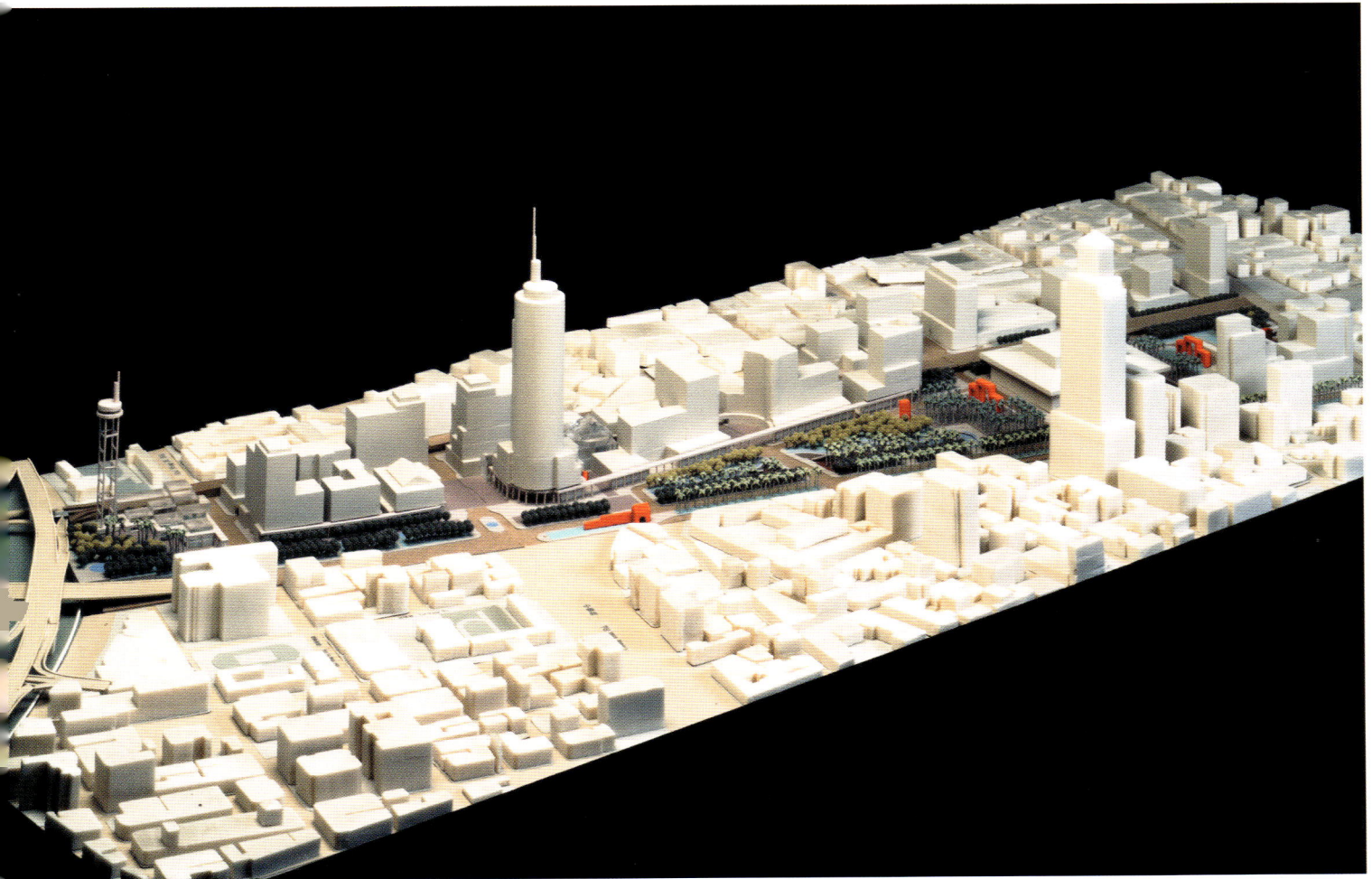

5

Beijing World Exhibition and Sports Center Planning

Competition 2000
Beijing, China
Joint-venture firms: Architecture Design Institute, Ministry of Construction Beijing,
Great Earth Architects & Engineers, International (Beijing),
Beyond Space Group, Architecture, Interior & Environment (Seoul)

Planning and Design Committee to Beijing World Exhibition and Sport Center

The Beijing World Exhibition and Sports Center is located on the central axis line of the north 4th and 5th ring roads of Beijing, occupying an area of 405 hectares. The purpose of planning such a center is to prepare to host the 2008 Olympic Games. It is an international competition, and this entry won the citation for design excellence.

Planning Concept

To expand the spine of Beijing's north–south grand central axis and place major buildings along the axis.

The layout of the Sports Center and Exhibition Center is to recognize and fix it into the contextual fabric of Beijing's city structure.

To create a northern end terminus of the grand north–south axis by placing the main stadium at the major intersection of the complex, and to place a juxtaposed super high-rise trade building at the northern end of the axis.

International Exhibition Center

The International Exhibition Center locates at the northern part of the land of the complex. Three high-rise buildings (the World Trade office building, a five-star hotel, and a luxury apartment building) line up on both sides of the central axis line, complementing and responding to the Bell & Drum Tower on the southern end of the central axis line, to reflect the characteristic of "extending the past into the future." Exhibition halls are situated on both sides of the central axis line, leaving the axis itself as an open plaza to deliver a unique urban space. This grand space functions as the gateway to the complex as well as to Beijing.

Sports Center Complex

The Sports Center Complex houses a total of 11 sports stadia for different sports functions. The overall design is to integrate each independent arena as coherent sports center with a main cable-roof structure system. The main stadium and the other independent arenas are planned to create a unified spatial form, as well as to allow for the unique character of each facility.

A thin roof shell is designed to lessen the impact of the arena's huge massing. The weightless roof provides a feeling of floating above the green trees.

At both the southern and northern ends of the main gym are arched walkways to link the whole exhibition and sports center from south to north and through the entire site. A magnificent 600-meter, artificial island in the ecological park will give people a place to wander.

Olympic villages to house the athletes during the day are provided. In the northwest and southeast, the housing complex is designed with different housing types to accommodate different needs. It is also designed with the idea that these housing units will be put on the market for sale after the Games.

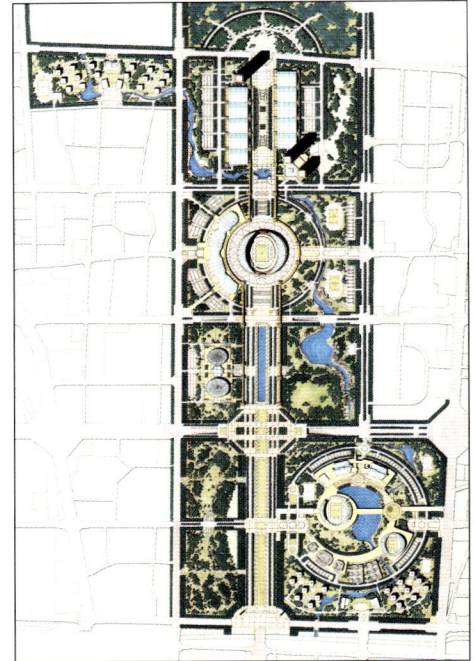

1

2

3

4

5

6

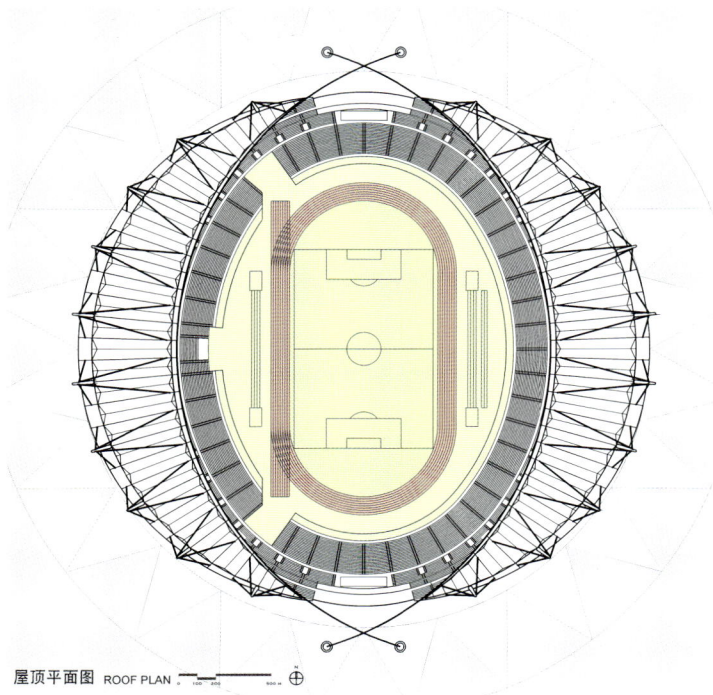

屋顶平面图 ROOF PLAN

7

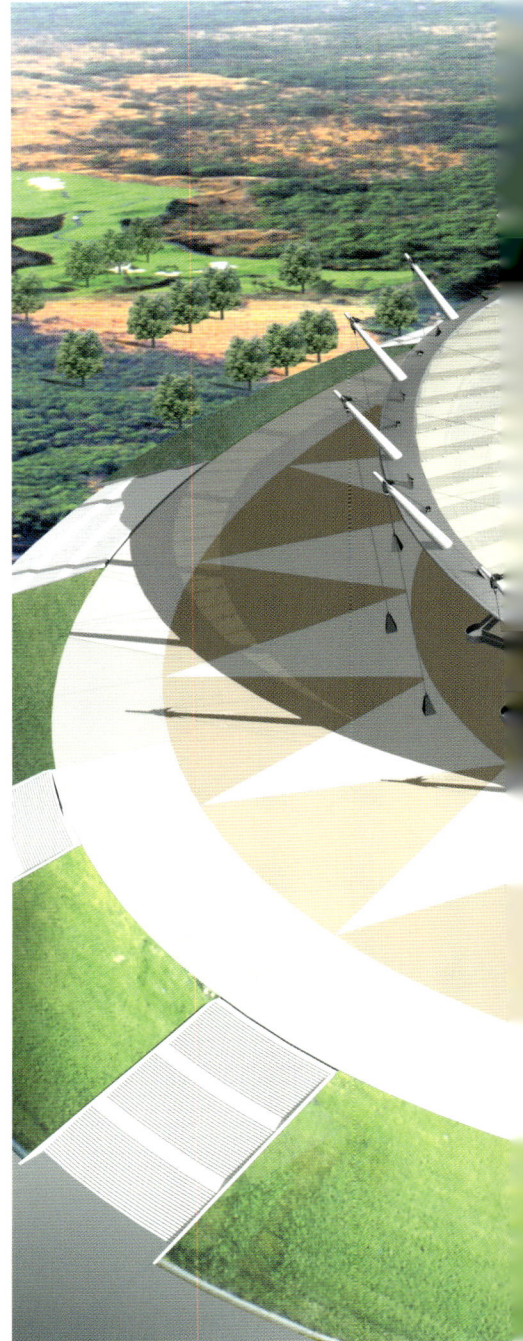

8

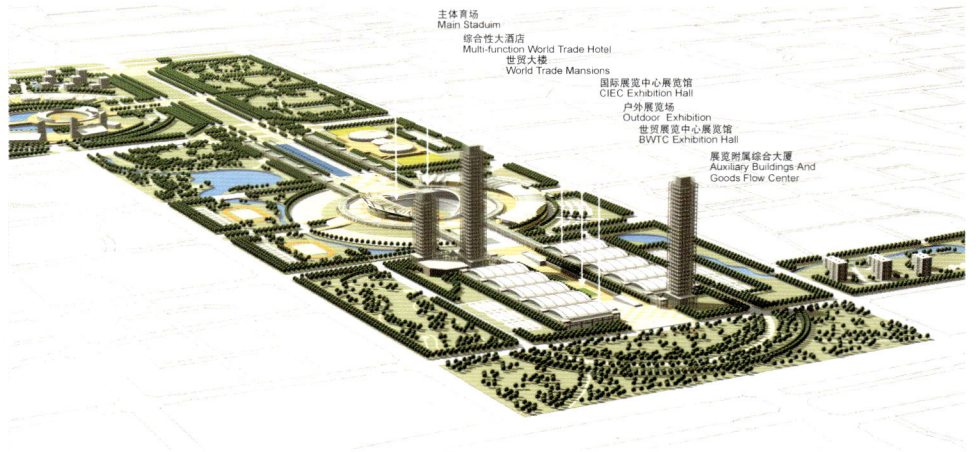

主体育场
Main Staduim
综合性大酒店
Multi-function World Trade Hotel
世贸大楼
World Trade Mansions
国际展览中心展览馆
CIEC Exhibition Hall
户外展览场
Outdoor Exhibition
世贸展览中心展览馆
BWTC Exhibition Hall
展览附属综合大厦
Auxiliary Buildings And
Goods Flow Center

10

11

Taipei Shwan-Lian Performance Art District and Urban Design

Planning/Completion 1997/1998
Taipei, Taiwan
Taipei City Government
1.04 hectares
Urban planning, urban design, tendering, operation management

In order to resolve the lack of sufficient performance art venues in the city today, Taipei City's Department of Urban Development is planning to create a "Performance Art District" in Taipei City's Shwan-Lian District. This district will integrate the stretch of leisure and arts facilities on Chung Shan N. Road, which include the Children's Amusement Park, Taipei Fine Arts Museum, Numbers 14 and 15 Parks, as well as the Chiang Kei-Shek Memorial Hall, making it the center of Taipei's arts, leisure, and entertainment activities.

The project includes both "performance" and "commercial" facilities. Performance art facilities will include a large and a medium-sized performance hall, a stage theater, rehearsal chamber, special arts library, and performance walkway. Space will also be provided for the Taipei Municipal Chinese Classical Orchestra. Commercial facilities include shops, art galleries, movie theaters, restaurants etc.

Development plans are divided into different area, such as a performance area, an open space area, and a high-density special commercial area. The northern and southern ends are the traditional residential areas. In order to connect the MRT stations with the arts and commercial facilities, an underground shopping arcade is provided.

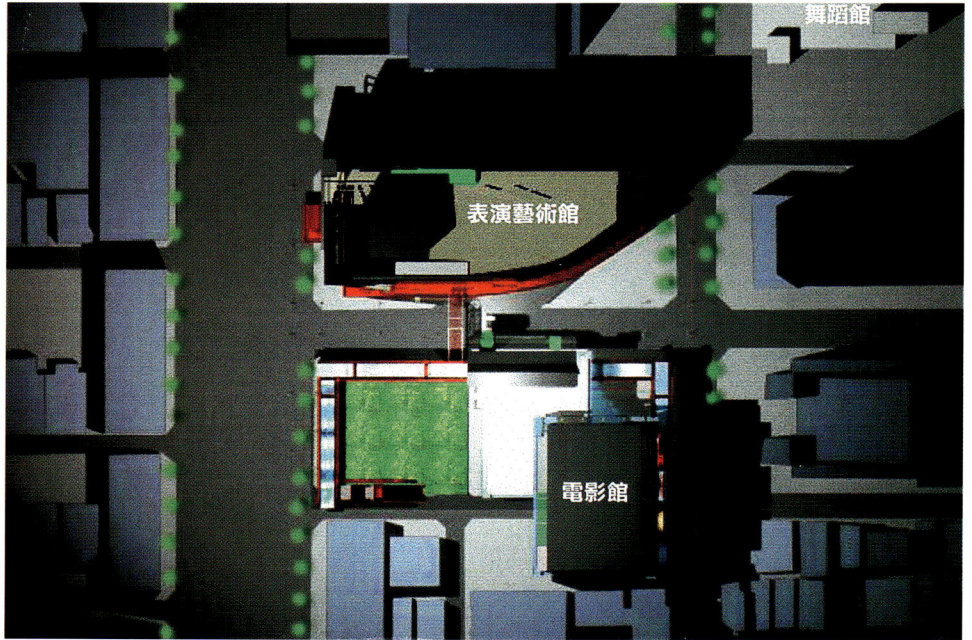

1

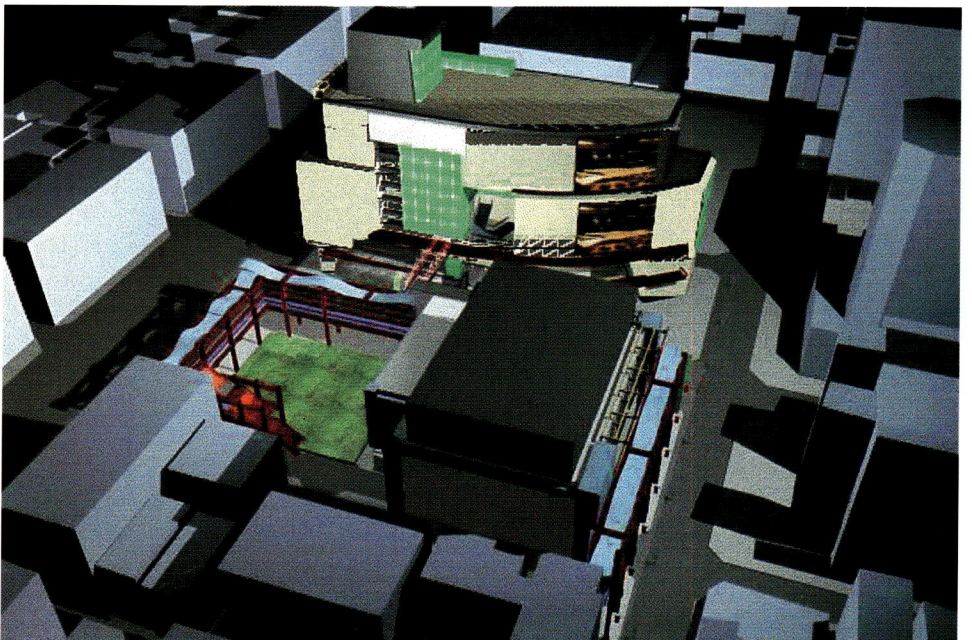

2

216

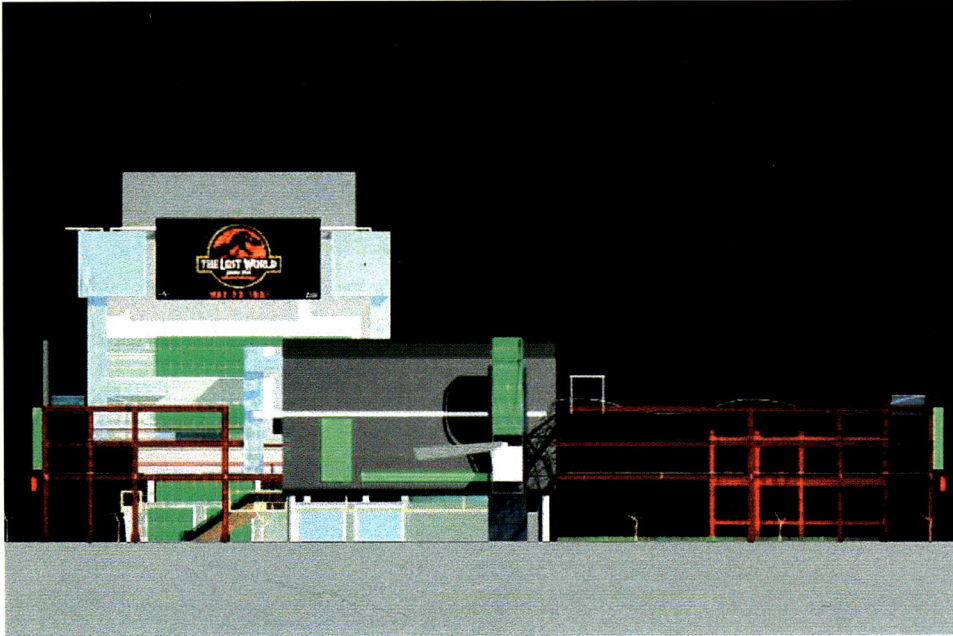

3

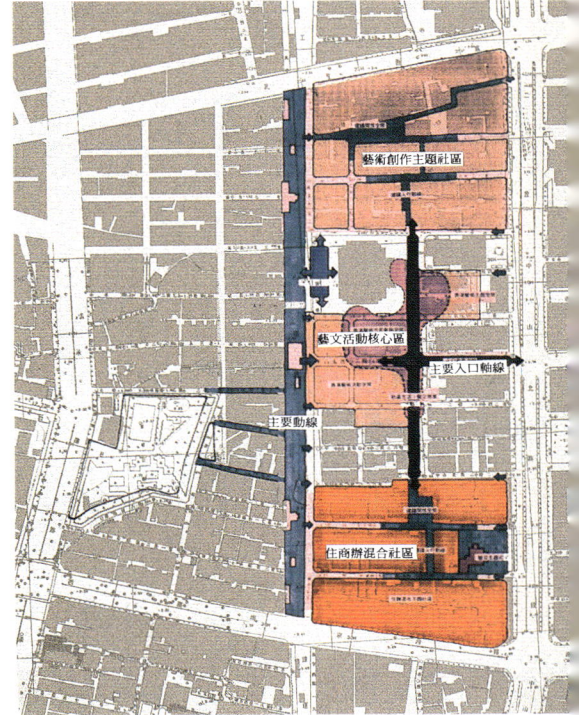

5

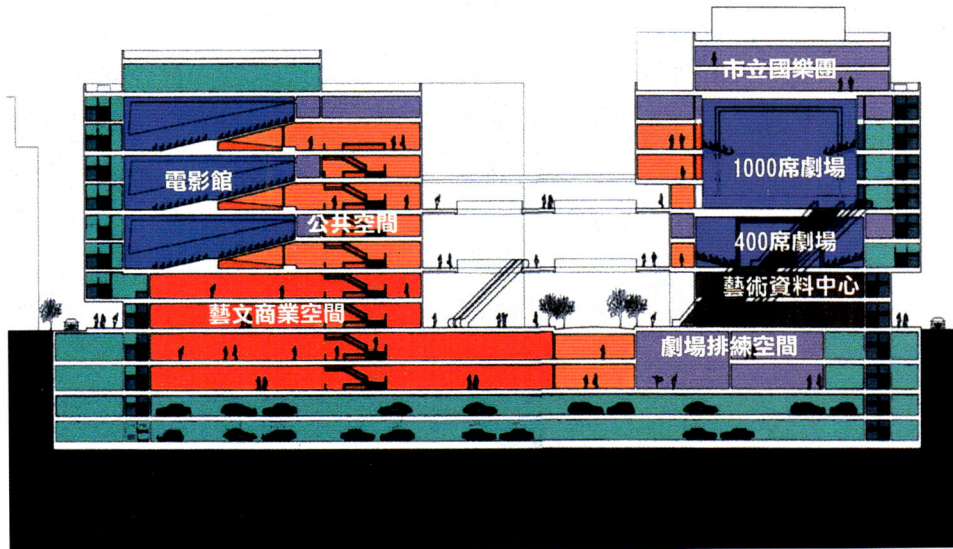

電影館
公共空間
藝文商業空間

市立國樂團
1000席劇場
400席劇場
藝術資料中心
劇場排練空間

4

1   District central area
2   Perspective of district center
3   Elevation of stage theater
4   Section of performance hall and stage theater
5   District zoning plan

Multi-functional Commerce and Trade Park

Comprehensive Plan and Rezoning, Kaoshiung
Planning/Completion 1996/1999
Kaohsiung City Government
587 hectares

In order to promote Taiwan as the operational hub of the Asia–Pacific region, in 1995 the Executive Yuan approved the export processing transformation project to be the main project in the first stage of promoting Taiwan. At the same time, the Harbor Bureau drafted the development project of Kaohsiung Harbor with the aim of improving the efficiency and functions of harbor facilities. Therefore, with these two projects in mind, the Kaohsiung government allocated the area close to the harbor for the Kaohsiung Multi-functional Commerce and Trade Park. Meanwhile, this project has been classified as a major development project for the future of Kaohsiung, in order for it to become a manufacturing center, as well as a sea-transportation center, to meet the criteria of becoming the Asia–Pacific Operation Hub.

In addition, since the growth and decline of a city is closely linked with the redevelopment of city land, how to use the land for a more efficient development has become a major issue for consideration. In order to address the problem of improper use of industrial land in Kaohsiung, the city government has decided to go along with the City Renewal Project put forth by the Executive Yuan to plan related details. The scope of this plan is also included in the areas of priority for the Executive Yuan.

Kaohsiung metropolitan area sets its comprehensive development goals in developing the city into a harbor metropolis to attract the investment of both transnational and domestic companies. Moreover, in order to make Taiwan the Asia–Pacific Operation Hub and to renovate Kaohsiung, the city government will realize the plan of building Kaohsiung into a multi-functional commerce and trade park, and will adjust the city function and structure of Kaohsiung. We hope that with this project and other related plans we will be able to build an international image for Kaohsiung and sufficiently use the land.

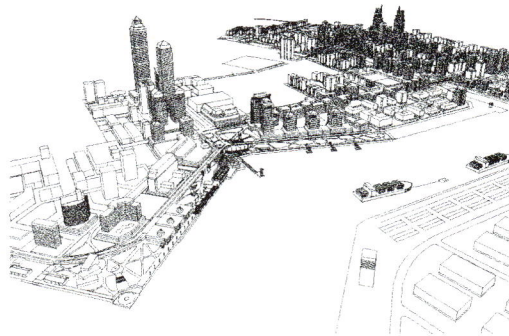

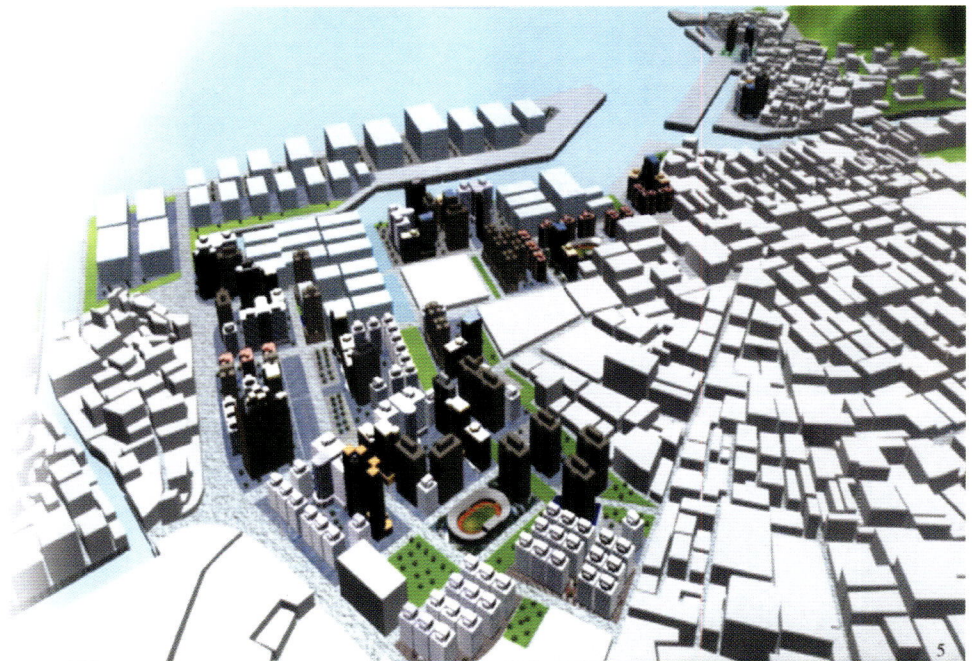

1   Perspective of harbor
2   Rendering of the Multi-functional Commerce and Trade Park
3   Zoning plan

Kaohsiung Harbor Bureau

Wu-fu Rd.

Chung-shan Rd.

Chen-kong Rd.

Shan-dow Rd.

Asia Enterprise
Center, 103 FL.

Tuntex 85 International
Plaza, 85FL.

Kaohsiung Harbor

New Administration
Building of Kaohsiung
Harbor Bureau

1st Containers
Center

Chung-hwa Rd.

特文一
特文二
特文三
特
文
特賢一
特賢二
四
特賢三
特倉三
特倉三
特倉三
特倉一
特倉二
特倉二
特倉二
特倉一
工37
特賢四
特賢四
商四
特賢四
特賢四
特賢五
特賢五
特賢五
特賢六
特賢六
特賢六
特倉一
特倉一

3

Firm Profile

Senior Staff: (Seated, left to right); W.C. Cheng, James C.C. Kuo, Anton R.T. Tsai, Haigo T.H. Shen, S.L. Chen, Chin Pai, Jin Xiu Ho, (Standing, left to right); T.L. Chen, J.J. Yu, S.C. Jao, S.Y. Wang, T.W. Lin, Ti Wai Shih, Nelson N.H. Shen, W.J. Teng, Albert Kao

Firm Profile

Haigo Shen & Associates, one of the leading and most established architectural firms in Taiwan, was formed in 1958. Within 42 years it has grown steadily from a staff of five to more than 200 personnel. For over two decades it has been recognized as the leader in its field in Taiwan. The diversity and complexity of its body of works and the increasing scale of the architectural and planning projects of the firm reflect the development and growth of Taiwan during the past 40 years.

The firm is widely recognized for design building in a straight forward manner and its level of professional competence. The body of works covers a wide range: one is struck by the diversity of project types that come from the office. These include some of Taiwan's largest hospitals and modern research facilities, university campuses, art museums, landmark hotels, residential complexes for different levels, urban rapid transit and high-speed rail facilities, large shopping centers and manufacturing facilities, and a large-scale sporting complex. In addition, the firm has contributed to the shaping of the urban environment in Taiwan, with its involvement in the urban design and planning of some pioneer projects, such as the Taipei Terminal Special District Urban Design, The Kaohsiung Rail Terminal Area Urban Design, the Kaohsiung Multi-Function Economic and Trade Park, Planning and the Restoration of the Chinbi Village in Matsu. These planning and urban design works have a great impact on the future of the urban environment in Taiwan.

In 1999, due to an increase in workload, the demands for frequent client contact and the need to upgrade professional services, Haigo Shen & Associates was re-organized and became Haigo Shen & Partners (HSP). It aims to provide a bridge to better service and to coordinating projects both locally and internationally.

The firm, aside from projects in Taiwan, also has extensive experience abroad, primarily in Singapore, Indonesia, Guam, Thailand, Honolulu, and China. The firm has also collaborated with many well-known international offices from Japan, the United States, England, Australia, Hong Kong, and Singapore. Due to the increased demand for architectural services in mainland China, branch offices of HSP have been established in Shanghai and Beijing to echo the rapid economic growth of the Chinese cities and to broaden the scope of professional services in the future.

Biographies

Haigo T.H. Shen
Founding Partner

Haigo Shen, who was honored by the American Institute of Architects as an Honorary Fellow of the Institute in the year 2000, is a leading architect in Taiwan and Asia. He celebrated the 40th anniversary of his establishment of his professional practice in the same year. Shen's accomplishments are reflected not only in his numerous award-winning buildings, but also in his leadership in advancing the standards of architectural education training and practice in Taiwan.

As the leading architectural office in Taiwan, Haigo Shen has established a well-organized office with 200 employees. He has maintained a high standard in design and in the development of construction documents, which are much sought after for their many practical aspects. Shen's office became the training ground for young architects in Taiwan. Haigo Shen had advanced changes in legislation to modernize the regulation of Taiwan, permitting the incorporation of an architectural company. He is the founder of the Taipei Architects Association, and was elected as its first president 30 years ago.

A pioneer in his own field, Shen designed the first modern office tower in Taipei in 1958, on Chung Shan North Road—a landmark building leading the way to the modern architectural era. With the vigorous economic growth in the 1960s and 70s in Taipei, Shen built the first apartment, the first television station, the first export processing zone, and the first assembly plant in Hsinchu Science-based Industrial Park. In the 1980s and 90s he collaborated with well-known international architects such as Kenzo Tange, Michael Graves, RMJM, HOK, PCF, RTKL for architectural and planning projects throughout Taiwan. One can say that the past 40 years' works of Haigo Shen reflect all aspects of the economic and urban development of Taiwan.

Haigo Shen believes the advancement of architecture begins with education. In the past years he has encouraged young architectural professionals by providing job opportunities as well as financial support. In view of this long-term commitment, in 1998 he established the Haigo Shen Architectural Education Foundation to provide scholarships for young professionals, to invite prominent international architects to participate in the Foundation Lecture series, and to publish books on architectural design and research.

As a leader in the field as well as the community, Haigo Shen is well respected for his participation in the numerous activities of different organizations, academic, professional, religious, and governmental. He has been a board of directors of T.Y. Lin International, St. John's & St. Mary's Institute of Technology, The Chinese Institute of Engineers, Tunghai University, and from 1988–1997 he was Honorary Consul, Embassy of Costa Rica. A person whose contributions and influences can be felt in every part of the community.

Haigo Shen graduated from St. John's University, Shanghai with a B.S. in Architectural Engineering. He was awarded a grant to undertake special study at the University of Michigan and at East-West Center, University of Hawaii in Honolulu.

Mark S.Y. Chan
Senior Partner

Mark S.Y. Chan, currently the senior partner of Haigo Shen & Partners, is one of the individuals who has contributed significantly to our firm's continued leadership in the field. Through his projects he has helped to raise architectural practice in Taiwan to meet the highest levels of international standards, and through his teaching of architecture at university departments of architecture he has worked to develop his profession. Within Haigo Shen & Partners, Chan has worked actively to develop higher levels of quality control through out the entire design process, as well to increase the efficiency and motivation within the organization.

An international viewpoint was formed early in Chan's career, beginning after he was awarded a master degree in architecture from Cheng Kung University in 1970 and moved to Hong Kong, where he practiced architecture for five years. Then, turning to the United States, he was awarded a Master of Architecture and Urban Design from Washington University, St. Louis in 1977, remaining to work in the United States for another two years.

Returning to Taiwan, Chan won the design competition for the new National Central Library, the first major library to be built in Taiwan, with a site located in the governmental and symbolic heart of Taipei City. Acting as director in charge of both design and construction supervision, Chan was responsible for a project that helped give new direction to modern architecture in Taiwan, and was recognized by *Architect Magazine's* 1985 Design Award, the first of many that his buildings have received. Subsequently, he has been responsible for numerous equally distinguished projects, many of which have had overseas clients or used foreign consulting firms for specialized engineering. For example, there is the Taipei American School, a six-hectare project providing an academic campus for 1,800 students over 12 grades, including a 600-seat auditorium, library, natatorium, gymnasium, and playing fields. Chan has also been responsible for a number of industrial projects, including the China Times Headquarters, Taipei's first major modern printing facility, which also includes office, exhibition, and performance spaces. Laboratory buildings which he has directed include the Information Science Research Laboratory at the Academia Sinica and the Chinese Medical Laboratories, the first of its kind in Taiwan. Retail projects include the Asia Plaza in Kaohsiung, a three-phase, mixed-use project, whose final phase will include a 103-story office building.

In the design of his projects, Mark Chan focuses on three areas: first, understanding and responding to the client's needs and program; second, developing an integrated design vision from the urban scale down to interior details; and third, keeping tight control of design quality, budget, and project schedule. Doing so, he has worked to develop an architecture that is free from temporary fashions and that responds flexibly to the individual clients and the wholistic contexts of their buildings. That his buildings have over time proved so satisfactory to both the clients and the public is clear testimony to the success of his balanced design and management philosophy.

Chin Pai
Senior Partner

A senior partner of Haigo Shen & Partners (HSP), Dr. Pai is also the director of planning and urban design of the affiliate office of Haigo Shen International Engineering Consultants Inc. Dr. Pai has an extensive professional and educational background in architecture and urban design. He has served both the private and public sector on a professional basis, and has taught in several universities, both in Taiwan and abroad. Dr. Pai joined HSP in 1987 as president of the company. At HSP he is directing a wide range of projects in architecture and urban design, including the Main Library of National Taiwan University, the National Chung Cheng University Master Plan, the Hsinchu Science City Development Plan, the Taipei Rail Terminal Urban Design Plan, the Taipei MCTS Transit System Station Design and Joint Development Planning, and the Kaohsiung Multi-Function Economic and Trade Park Development Plan. He is very active as a planning and design consultant in China, directing a wide range of projects including a City Center Plan for Shekou, Shenzhen, the Huachiaocheng Plan in Shenzhen, and a Master Plan for the Xiamen Economic Zone in the People's Republic of China. Recently, he was the project director for the planning of the 2008 Olympic Sports Center and National Exhibition Center, a joint-venture project with the design institutes in Beijing which won a citation for design in the year 2000.

Dr. Pai was associated with DMJM, Doxiadis, Inc., the Rouse Company, Okamoto/Liskamm and SOM/The President's Commission on Pennsylvania Avenue in the USA, where he was responsible for the planning and design of many important urban design projects, including the Honolulu Rapid Transit System, the Georgetown Waterfront Plan, the Columbia and Reston New Town Plan, and the planning and implementation of the Pennsylvania Avenue Redevelopment Plan and the Mall Plan in Washington, D.C.

Dr. Pai's influence extends beyond his office. In addition to his professional experience he has taught in the United States, China, Singapore, and Taiwan. He was a professor and chairman of the School of Architecture at Tamkang University, Taipei and an associate professor and Chairman of the Postgraduate and Research Program at the National University of Singapore. He was a research fellow of the Advanced Studies Program of the National Academy of Science of the United States to conduct research in China, and an exchange scholar between the University of Michigan and Tsinghua University in Beijing. He has taught at Carnegie-Mellon University, the University of Michigan, and has been a visiting professor, critic and juror at many universities including MIT, Harvard GSD, the University of Tokyo, the Chinese University of Hong Kong, National Taiwan University, National Cheng Kung University, Tunghai University, and Shanghai University.

Dr. Pai has been very active in providing government and community services. He was a member of the mayor of Honolulu's urban design task force and an advisor to the Department of Urban Development of Honolulu, 1974–76. He was also an urban development advisor to the mayor of Taipei from 1996 to 1998. He served as advisor to the Department of Housing and Urban Development of the Council for Economic and Construction of the Executive Yuan and the Tourism Bureau of the Ministry of Communication in Taiwan. He is a member of the American Institute of Certified Planners and an international member of the American Institute of Architects. He is also a member and was on the Board of Directors of the Chinese Architects Association, the Chinese Urban Planning Institute. Dr. Pai is the founder of the Chinese Institute of Urban Design in 1994 in Taiwan.

Dr. Pai graduated from National Cheng Kung University with a Bachelor of Architecture. He obtained a Master of Architecture and Urban Design from Washington University in St. Louis, a Master of Architecture from MIT, and a Doctorate in Architecture from the University of Michigan.

WITHDRAWN

Anton R.T. Tsai
Senior Partner

Anton Tsai graduated from the Architectural Engineering Department of National Cheng Kung University in 1969. He studied Passive Solar Energy and Architecture at the Massachusetts Institute of Technology in 1982 and was commissioned to design the Ambassadors for Christ Paradise Center in Pennsylvania in 1986. The following year he studied Uniform Building Code at the California Polytechnic University in Pomona and attended Tai-fu Seminary for his master's degree. He returned to Taiwan in 1991.

From 1969 to 1972 Tsai worked for Acropolis Architects & Planners, Engineers & Associates before he founded Rong-Tang Tsai Architects & Associates in 1972. From 1975 to 1980, he worked as the leading editor for *Chinese Architect*, an architectural magazine based in Taiwan. Tsai assisted in the evaluation and establishment of the Chinese version of *GA World Architecture* from 1983 to 1984, a publication whose volume totals 56 books. He served three terms on the board of directors of ROC Architect Association between the years of 1977 and 2000 and monitored the association's operations from 1979 till 1983. From 1983 to 1985 and 1997 to the present, he has been the supervisor on the board of directors of Taipei City Architect Association and Taiwan Architect Association. Furthermore, he served at the Ministry of Interior to do research on a team whose function was to define the responsibility scope of architectural designers and supervisors from 1980 to 1981.

In 1992, Tasi was the team leader in the design and supervision of construction of the College Chapel at the Tamsui Aletheia University. When the building was completed in 1997, he received an "excellent architect" award from the Taiwan Provincial Governor during the opening ceremony. Moreover, Tsai headed a team to design and supervise a big-scale project for the Tuntex Distinct Corp., which involved a complex of 32 buildings with 16 floors above ground and 4 floors underground in Ba-dou-zi, Keelung. In 1998, he cooperated with Kenzo Tange, a Japanese architect to compete in a competition with other eight renowned architects for designing the President International Tower in the Hsinyi district for Tainan group, a competition for which his team won the first place.

Tsai, an active member of the Taipei Committee for Architectural Law, is currently the legal consultant for the committee and is also the leader of "Researching How to Implement the System for Certifying and Checking Architect Qualification," a project commissioned by the Taipei City Government. In addition, he is a member of technical review for information integration and construction guidelines under the Public Construction Committee of the Executive Yuan, a committee member to review construction licenses for the Keelung City Government, and a committee member to review and provide consultation to the Taipei City Government regarding how to make public buildings improve facilities of the disabled.

After the 9/21/'99 earthquake, Tsai participated in the recovery work of the disastrous areas and was responsible for the designing, planning and supervision the reconstruction of Xu-guang Junior High School and Chun-liao Elementary School, Bei-mei Junior High, Kuang-fu Junior High and Kuang-fu Elementary School. At the present, he is leading the project to rebuild old military houses in Chiayi City and Taichung, commissioned by the Ministry of National Defense. Apart from his work, Tsai enjoys participating in the research of architectural art and charitable work of the Architect Association. His work has received much recognition in both Taiwan and Japan.

Jin-Xiu Ho
Partner

Jin-Xiu Ho graduated from Feng-Chia University in 1983, with a Bachelor of Arts degree in architecture. In 1991, she obtained her master degree in architecture from Harvard University.

Upon graduation, Ho worked for Fei & Cheng Associates for five years. During that period, she was involved in projects of architecture design and related fields. Ho has established a clear and complete process for architectural implementation, especially in her work on the design of National Museum of Natural Science, which was considered a breakthrough in her career development. Ho found the opportunity to integrate all the practical experience she had accumulated, from preliminary design, detailed design, and construction documents to subcontracting plans. In addition, the coordination experience with foreign consultants further expanded her perspectives on international cooperation. This was the most important time in Ho's career development, which provided the initiating period in the development of her professional capabilities in architecture.

The experience of study, work, and travel in the United States from 1989 to 1992 not only broadened Ho's knowledge and thoughts, but also helped to enhance her international views on architecture. This period had a tremendous influence on Ho's work on international architecture projects and urban designs.

After her return to Taiwan in 1992, Ho worked for Liu & Associates, whose architectural design projects were mostly private development projects. The experience provided her with the executive abilities in architecture design, urban design, and planning for both the public and the private sectors. During this critical period, she obtained overall and practical and capabilities in the architecture field, which also created a solid foundation in preparing for her to be in a senior position in an architecture practice.

Ho started working for Haigo Shen & Partners in 1998, and was in charge of one of the four design departments, which was involved in a number of major architectural projects and cooperation with many well-known international architects. Ho has guided her department toward a direction of international perspectives.

As a partner of HSP, Ho has had great responsibilities and has broadened her architectural career. In recruiting young talented architects to join HSP, she has contributed in making the company a leading architectural company in Taiwan.

Nelson N.H. Shen
Architect

Mr. Nelson Shen was born in 1960 at Hsinchu, Taiwan. In 1983, he graduated from the Department of Architecture of Chung-Yuan University. From 1989 to 1990, he studied at the University of Colorado, Denver, where he was awarded a master degree in building technology.

After graduating from the university, Mr. Shen worked for the Urban Development Bureau of Taipei City Government. His major involvement was participating in urban-design related work and preliminary planning of the underground mall of Chung-hwa Road. In urban design, he focused on the work of The Hsin-Yi District and The old river way in Shih-lin area. The underground mall of Chung-hwa Road is now under construction, and MRT Taipei Mall currently in use is part of the project. Mr. Shen sees the opportunity to participate in these two projects as very precious. They have played an important role in the development of his career.

In 1990, Mr. Shen returned to Taiwan and joined the Urban Planning Department at Haigo Shen & Associates. His major task focused on large-scale land development. In the following five years, he participated in major projects such as Redevelopment Plan of Peng-lai Business District in Kaoshiung, overall design and planning of Sun Yat-San Art District in Taipei, use and planning of land becoming available as the a result of railroads going underground in Taipei, land development of Hei-song's Taipei plant, and land development of Feng-shan Gung-wu for Tai-sugar. In addition to urban planning and design, Mr. Shen also assisted in market analysis, financial planning, and operation management of all these projects. Through the process of meetings and consultation, Mr. Shen has accumulated additional experience in project analysis and management.

1993 was Mr. Shen's third year with the firm. He was selected by his department to attend an international architecture forum (IFYA) held in Kobe by the International Academy of Architecture (IAA). The seminar lasted for 10 days. During this time, he had the opportunity to work with young architects from Japan and Mexico. Moreover, their team competed against seven teams formed by architects from countries around the world. Mr. Shen's team won the first prize and Kobe Mayor's Award. Currently, Mr. Shen is a member of IAA and activities of this sort are still going on around the world.

This year marks the sixth year for Mr. Shen at the firm. He has always been involved in work related to architectural design and construction. He has participated in projects such as Student Center of Business Administration Department at National Cheng-Chih University, Taiwan Life Insurance Building in Taichung, Si-Chi Distribution Center for Tait group of companies, Classroom Building for Yu-Chen Senior High School in Taipei, President Group Hsin-Yi Headquarters Building, and Ocean Park and Resort Hotel in Hualien. From planning to design and construction, Mr. Shen participates in every detail. In addition, many international cooperation projects have further increased Mr. Shen's ability and knowledge in the field of architecture.

Mr. Shen views architecture as activities of creation and production, and designing is an important part of these activities. A good piece of work usually comes from a rich life experience. A successful creation can almost be seen as an invention. For Mr. Shen, life can be routine, but architectural output definitely must be extraordinary.

Chronological List of Buildings and Projects

* Indicates work featured in this book (see Selected and Current Works)

Education

* Library and Information Center,
National Chiayi University
2000–2004
Chiayi, Taiwan
National Chiayi University

* Sports Center, National Taiwan
University
1994–2001
Taipei, Taiwan
National Taiwan University

* Library and Information Center ,
National Kaohsiung First University of
Science and Technology
1997–2001
Kaohsiung, Taiwan
National Kaohsiung First University of
Science and Technology

Chun-Liao Primary School
2000–2001
Nantou, Taiwan
TVBS caring for Taiwan Foundation

* Main Library, National Taiwan University
1990–1998
Taipei, Taiwan
National Taiwan University

* College of Business, National Cheng-
Chih University
1993–1997
Taipei, Taiwan
National Cheng-Chih University

* Assembly Hall, National Chung-Cheng
University
1990–1994
Chiayi, Taiwan
National Chung-Cheng University

* Classroom Building, National Chung-
Cheng University
1989–1991
Chiayi, Taiwan
National Chung-Cheng University

* Campus Planning, Academic Buildings
and Gymnasium, Taipei American School
1987–1989 (Phase I); 1988–1991 (Phase
II); 1987–1990 (Gymnasium)
Taipei, Taiwan
Taipei American School

Classroom Building, Chinese Culture
University
1989–1992
Taipei, Taiwan
Chinese Culture University

Economic Research Institute, National
Taiwan University
1982–1984
Taipei, Taiwan
National Taiwan University

Classroom for College of Literature,
National Taiwan University
1976–1977
Taipei, Taiwan
National Taiwan University

International Student Center, China Youth
Corps
1974–1977
Taipei, Taiwan
China Youth Corps

Institute Oceangraphy Building, National
Taiwan University
1967–1970
Taipei, Taiwan
National Taiwan University

Classroom Building, St. John's & St. Mary's
Institute of Technology
1965–1967
Tamsui, Taiwan
St. John's & St. Mary's Institute of
Technology

* Chapel, St. John's & St. Mary's Institute
of Technology
1965–1968
Tamsui, Taiwan
St. John's & St. Mary's Institute of
Technology

Public/Government

* Nantou County Municipal Building
2000–2002
Nantou, Taiwan
Nantou County Government

* The New Taichung City Civic Center
Competition
Taichung, Taiwan
Taichung City Government

Kaohsiung City Swimming Pool
1991–1996
Kaohsiung, Taiwan
Kaohsiung City Government

* Postal Processing Center, Kaohsiung
Competition
Kaohsiung, Taiwan
General Post Office

Min-Sheng District Community Center
1985–1989
Taipei, Taiwan
Taipei City Government

* Convention Center, Taipei World Trade
Center
1984–1989
Taipei, Taiwan
Ministry of Economic Affairs, Executive
Yuan

* Exhibition Center, Taipei World
Trade Center
1981–1985
Taipei, Taiwan
Ministry of Economic Affairs, Executive
Yuan
Joint Venture Firm: HOK, USA

Wine and Tobacco Monopoly Bureau
Taipei Warehouse
1986–1988
Taipei, Taiwan
Wine and Tobacco Monopoly Bureau

Hsinyi Housing/Office Building
1983–1988
Taipei, Taiwan
National Property Bureau, Ministry of
Finance

Yunlin County Municipal Building
1977–1978
Yunlin, Taiwan
Yunlin County Government
Joint Venture Firm: Victor Y.T. Chang
& Associates

Office Building, Ministry of Finance
1968–1970
Taipei, Taiwan
Ministry of Finance

Taipei Customs Office Building
1971–1973
Taipei, Taiwan
Ministry of Finance

Office Building, Central Weather Bureau
1969–1972
Taipei, Taiwan
Central Weather Bureau

Commercial/Office Building

* FE 21 Mega
1995–2001 (Phase I)
Kaohsiung, Taiwan
Yuan-Ding Construction Co., Ltd.
Joint Venture Firm: Wong & Ouyang (HK)
Ltd, Architects & Engineers

Chung-Bang Shopping Center
2000–2004
Taipei, Taiwan
Yuan-Ding Construction Co. Ltd
Joint Venture Firm: Kisho Kurokawa
Architect & Associates, Japan

* Taishin International Bank Building
1998–2004
Taipei, Taiwan
Taishin International Bank
Joint Venture Firm: Pei Cobb Freed &
Partners, USA

* President International Tower
1998–2003
Taipei, Taiwan
President Enterprises Group
Joint Venture Firm: Kenzo Tange
Associates, Japan

Wu-Ze Shopping Center
1998–2003
Taichung, Taiwan
Tai-Song Construction Co., Ltd.
Joint Venture Firm: RTKL, U.S.A.

* Nan-Shan Life Insurance Corporation
Headquarters
1997–2003
Taipei, Taiwan
Nan-Shan Life Insurance Co., Ltd.
Joint Venture Firm: C.F. Tong & Associates

* Emerald Rose Garden Hotel, Myanmar
1994–2002
Rangoon, Myanmar
Emerald Rose Garden Hotel Company

* Pan-German Motors Ltd Headquarters
1997–1999 (pending)
Taipei, Taiwan
Pan-German Motors Ltd.

* Grand Hyatt Hotel
1983–1989
Taipei, Taiwan
Hong-Leong Hotel Development Ltd.

Information Industrial Institute Building
1982–1988
Taipei, Taiwan
Ministry of Economic Affairs, Executive
Yuan

* Chung-Hsin Textile Company
Headquarters
1983–1986
Taipei, Taiwan
Chung-Hsin Textile Co. Ltd

Central Daily News Building
1983–1987
Taipei, Taiwan
Central Daily News

Empire Building
1982–1985
Taipei, Taiwan
Tung-Yun Co. Ltd

China International Commercial Bank,
Taichung Branch
1979–1981
Taichung, Taiwan
China International Commercial Bank

Taiping & First Life Commercial Building
1979–1981
Taipei, Taiwan
Taiping Life Insurance & First Life
Insurance Co. Ltd

Chang-Hwa Commercial Bank Building
1975–1978
Taipei, Taiwan
Chang-Hwa Commercial Bank
Joint Venture Firm: C.K. Chen & Associates

CAL Commercial Building
1977–1979
Taipei, Taiwan
China Airlines
Joint Venture Firm: Sam Chang &
Associates, USA

United Daily News Building
1969–1972
Taipei, Taiwan
United Daily News
Joint Venture Firm: W.T. Yang & Associates

Taipei Hilton Hotel
1967–1970
Taipei, Taiwan
Taipei Hilton Hotel

Reinsurance Building
1965–1967
Taipei, Taiwan

* Chia-Hsin Building
1964–1967
Taipei, Taiwan
Chia-Hsin Cement Company
Joint Venture Firm: Eric Cumine &
Associates, Hong Kong

Recreation/Culture

* National Museum of Prehistory
1993–2001
Taitung, Taiwan
National Museum of Prehistory
Joint Venture Firm: Michael Graves
& Associates

* National Museum of Marine Biology &
Aquarium
1990–2000 (Phase I); 1990–2001 (Phase II)
Pingtung, Taiwan
National Museum of Marine Biology and
Aquarium
Joint Venture Firm: KCMI, USA/J.J. Pan
& Partners

* Yamay Discovery World Water Park
1999–2000
Taichung, Taiwan
Yamay International Development Co. Ltd

* Ocean Park & Farest Resort Hotel,
Hualien
1997–2002
Hualien, Taiwan
Metropolitan Construction Co. Ltd
Joint Venture Firm: Alan Griffith Architects
(Overall site conceptual design and the
specialist design architect for the Marine
Park)
Resort: Wimberly Allison Tong & Goo,
USA

Great Penghu International Resort
1999–2002
Penghu, Taiwan
Penghu Bay Development Co. Ltd
Joint Venture Firm: Wimberly Allison Tong
& Goo, USA

* Kaohsiung Arena
Competition
Kaohsiung, Taiwan
Kaohsiung City Government

Ming Lake Resort
1995–2003
Miaoli, Taiwan
Nan-Jung Amusement Development Co.
Ltd

The First Golf Course & Club
1986–1989
Taoyuan, Taiwan
Kuo-Sheng Amusement Co. Ltd

* National Museum of Taiwan History
Competition
Tainan, Taiwan
The Preparatory Office of National
Museum of Taiwan History

Transportation

Mucha Extention (Neihu) line BR1 Station
2001–2007
Taipei, Taiwan
Department of Rapid Transit Systems,
Taipei City Government

Taiwan High Speed Rail Depots – Main
Workshop
Chiaotou, Taiwan
2001–2004
Taiwan High Speed Rail Corporation

Taiwan High Speed Rail Taoyuan Station
Taoyuan, Taiwan
1999–2005
Taiwan High Speed Rail Corporation
Joint Venture Firm: RMJM Hong Kong
Limited

* MCTS Transit Station, Taipei
1988–1996 (total 12 stations)
Taipei, Taiwan
Taipei City Government
Joint Venture Firm: T.Y. Lin Taiwan
Consulting Engineers, Inc.; MATRA Inc.

* Taipei Main Station
1984–1989
Taipei, Taiwan
Engineering Office of Taipei Railway
Underground Project, Ministry of
Transportation and Communications
Joint Venture Firm: C.K. Chen &
Associates; KMG Architects & Engineers,
Japan

* Harbor Terminal and Visitor Center,
Taichung
Competition
Taichung, Taiwan
Taichung Harbor Bureau

* Terminal Building, Taipei International
Airport
1969–1970
Taipei, Taiwan
Civil Aeronautic Administration
Joint Venture: C.K. Chen & Associates, Da-
Hong Wong & Associates

Civil Aeronautic Administration Office
Building
1971–1975
Taipei, Taiwan
Civil Aeronautic Administration
Joint Venture: Sam Chang & Associates,
USA

Industrial

Flytech Technology Office/Factory
Complex
2000–2003
Taipei, Taiwan
Flytech Technology Co., Ltd.

* Yageo Corporation Kaohsiung Factory III
1998–2001
Kaohsiung, Taiwan
Yageo Corporation

* Alpha Telecom Inc., New Facility
1995–1997
Hsinchu, Taiwan
Alpha Telecom Inc.

* Sunplus Technology Corporation –
Office/Factory Complex
1995–1996
Hsinchu, Taiwan
Sunplus Technology Corporation

Hua-Hsan Air Caters
1994–1996
Taoyuan, Taiwan
Cathay Pacific Catering Services

Walsin Technology Corporation –
Office/Factory Complex
1996–1999
Yangmei, Taiwan
Walsin Technology Corporation

Texas Instruments Taiwan Ltd, New
Factory
1993–1995
Chungho, Taiwan
Texas Instruments Taiwan Ltd

Kodak Operation Building
1984–1986
Peitou, Taiwan
Kodak Color Processing Inc.

Parke-Davis Corp. New Plant
1980–1982
Neili, Taiwan
Parke-Davis Corporation

Johnson & Johnson Plant
1981–1983
Hukou, Taiwan
Johnson & Johnson Co. Ltd

Dow Corning Plant
1981–1982
Chungli, Taiwan
Dow Corning Co. Ltd

Yue-Loong New Plant
1978–1980
Miaoli, Taiwan
Yue-Loong Motor Company

Toyota Motor Plant
1986–1988
Chungli, Taiwan
TOYOTA Motor Company

Nantze Export Processing Zone Planning,
Offices, Facilities, Roads, Drainages and
Standard Factory Buildings
1970–1973
Nantze, Taiwan
Ministry of Economic Affairs
Joint Venture Firm: CTCI

Taichung Export Processing Zone
Planning, Standard Factory Buildings, 1st
and 2nd stage
1969–1972
Taichung, Taiwan
Ministry of Economic Affairs
Joint Venture Firm: CTCI

Research/Medical

Mercy Hospital
1997–1999
Yunlin, Taiwan
Tze-Lien Enterprises Company

* Cancer Center, Koo Foundation
1992–1997
Taipei, Taiwan
Koo Foundation
Joint Venture Firm: NBBJ, U.S.A.

* Institute of Biomedical Sciences,
Academia Sinica
1989–1995
Taipei, Taiwan
Academia Sinica

* Institute of Modern History, Academia
Sinica
1989–1993
Taipei, Taiwan
Academia Sinica

Kaohsiung Veteran General Hospital
1985–1987
Kaohsiung, Taiwan
RET Service Engineering Agency
Joint Venture Firm: Fei Cheng & Assocites,
H.C. Hwang Partners, Inc., USA

Religious

* College Chapel, Tamsui Aletheia University
1993–1997
Tamsui, Taiwan
Tamsui Aletheia University

* Chapel, St. John's & St. Mary's Institute of Technology
1967–1968
Tamsui, Taiwan
St. John's & St. Mary's Institute of Technology

* Good Shepherd Church
1965–1967
Shihlin, Taiwan
Taiwan Episcopal Church

Housing

* Green Village
1997–2001
Hsintien, Taiwan
Continental Engineering Corporation

Tuntex Community Housing
1990–1999
Keelung, Taiwan
Tuntex Distinct Corporation

* Cheng-Kung Village Community Housing Project
1980–1984
Taipei, Taiwan
Taipei City Government

Ten-Mu Condominium
1980–1982
Tenmu, Taiwan
Lu Chang-Tong

Szu-Wei Community Housing Project
1976–1980
Kaohsiung, Taiwan
Kaohsiung City Government

Park Mansions
1972–1974
Taipei, Taiwan
Cathay Life Insurance Company

Union Villa II, 1,100 Units Low Cost Apartments and Community Planning
1964–1965
Taipei, Taiwan
United Builders

Planning

Guangzhou New Baiyun International Airport
South Working District Planning
2001
Guangzhou, China
Guangzhou Gaiyun International Airport Headquarters

* Beijing World Exhibition and Sports Center Planning
2000
Beijing Planning and Design Committee International Planning and Design Open Consultation
Joint-venture Firm: Architecture Design Institute, Ministry of Construction (Beijing); Great Earth Architects & Engineers, International (Beijing); Beyond Space Group, Architecture, Interior & Environment, Korea

* Kaohsiung Multi-functional Commerce &Trade Park Comprehensive Plan and Rezoning
1996–1999
Kaohsiung, Taiwan
Kaohsiung City Government

* Taipei Shwan-Lien Performance Art District and Urban Design
1997–1998
Taipei, Taiwan
Taipei City Government

* Campus Planning, National Chung-Cheng University
1988–1991
Chiayi, Taiwan
National Chung-Cheng University

* Taipei Terminal Special District Urban Design and Planning
1989–1990
Taipei, Taiwan
Taipei City Government
Joint Venture Firm: Sasaki, USA

TV & Broadcasting Facilities

TTV Studio, Offices, Auditorium, Transmitter and Relay Stations
1962–1964
Taipei, Taiwan
Taiwan Television Enterprise, Ltd

CTV Studio, Offices, Auditoriums
1969–1971
Taipei, Taiwan
China Television Company, Taipei

CTS Studio, Offices, Auditoriums, Training School, Transmitter and Relay Stations
1970–1972
Taipei, Taiwan
China Television Service, Ltd

Awards and Exhibitions

Awards

Grand Award
American Consulting Engineers Council
(ACEC) 2001 Engineering Excellence
Awards Competition
National Museum of Marine Biology and
Aquarium, Pingtung
Taiwan
2001

Quality Excellence Award
National Public Construction Annual
Award
National Museum of Marine Biology and
Aquarium, Pingtung
Taiwan
1999

**Construction Quality Excellence
Award**
Ministry of Education Award
National Museum of Prehistory, Taitung
Taiwan
1999

AIA Columbus Chapter Design Award
Cancer Center, Koo Foundation
1999

**Taiwan Provincial Government
Building Design Award**
Religious Architecture/ College Chapel,
Tamsui Oxford University
Taiwan
1998

**The Third R.O.C. Outstanding
Architectural Planning and Design
Contribution Award**
Ministry of Interior Award
Religious Architecture/ College Chapel,
Tamsui Oxford University
Taiwan
1997

Quality Excellence Award
National Public Construction Annual
Award
College of Business, National Cheng-Chih
University
Taiwan
1996

**National Building Design Award for
Passive Energy Efficiency**
Ministry of Interior Design Award
Campus Planning and Classroom, Taipei
American School
Taiwan
1996

**National Building Contribution Award
for Passive Energy Efficiency**
Ministry of Interior Award
Grand Hyatt Hotel
Taiwan
1996

**National Building Design Award for
Passive Energy Efficiency**
Ministry of Interior Award
Grand Hyatt Hotel
Taiwan
1992

**The 13th R.O.C. Design Silver Plaque
Award**
Taiwan Architect Association Annual
Design Award
Taipei World Trade International
Convention Center
Taiwan
1991

Annual Award of Excellence
American Society of Landscape Architects
Taipei Station Special Use District Urban
Design Guidelines
Taiwan

**Taipei Municipal Building Design
Award**
Taipei World Trade Exhibition Center
Taiwan
1986

The 8th R.O.C. Design Special Award
Taiwan Architects Association Annual
Design Award
Taipei World Trade Exhibition Center
Taiwan
1986

**Taipei Municipal Construction
Excellence Award**
The Empire Building
Taiwan
1985

Exhibitions

**Theme Works—A Design Symposium
on Themed Environments**
Hong Kong Convention and Exhibition
Center
October 2000

**The 1st Shanghai International
Architectural Design Exhibition**
Shanghai Mart
January 2000

**The Exhibition of the 3rd and 4th
R.O.C. Outstanding Architects Award
Recipients**
National Museum of History
April—June 1999

Acknowledgments

Haigo Shen & Partners wish to take this opportunity to express our gratitude and give our sincere thanks to our colleagues, collaborators, clients, and friends who have contributed to the firm's body of work over the years. They are:

Alan Griffith (Architect) Pty Ltd

Asian Technical Consultants, Inc.

Bechtel Corporation

Chia-Fan Tong & Associates

Chi-Kuan Chen Architect

Carol R. Johnson Associates, Inc.

Chermayeff, Sollogub and Poole, Inc.

Da-Hong Wong & Associates

E & C Engineering Corporation

Esherick, Homsey Dodge and David (EHDD)

Evergreen Consulting Engineering, Inc.

Gen-Yeh Engineering Consultants Inc.

H.M. Brandston & Partners, Inc., Taiwan

Hellmuth, Obata & Kassabaum, Inc. (HOK)

J.J. Pan & Partners

KCM International Inc.

Kenzo Tange Associates, Urbanists–Architects

Kisho Kurokawa Architect & Associates

KMG Architect

Michael Graves & Associates

Moh and Associates, Inc.

NBBJ

Parsons Brinckerhoff International, (Pte) Ltd

Pei Cobb Freed & Partners Architects

RMJM Hong Kong Limited

RTKL Associates Inc.

Sasaki Associates

Sasaki Walker Associates (SWA)

T.Y. Lin Taiwan Consulting Engineers, Inc.

Wimberly Allison Tong & Goo, Architects, Planners and Consultants

Wong & Ouyang (HK) Ltd, Architects and Engineers

Weathered Howe Pty Ltd

From all the firm's partners, we wish to thank the following people whose dedicated efforts have made this book possible. Ms Cassy Cheng, the project manager for this publishing venture, liaised with all parties involved to make it happen. Ms T.S. Lai, editor of this monograph; her patient and meticulous efforts in putting this book together has finally paid off. Ms Maggie Pai, the English editor who possesses not only good language skills but also knowledge in architecture; her exhaustive editing work is most valuable. Many others also provided help in the making of this book, including Nan-Cheih Wu, J.J. Yu, Ching-Chuan Liao, Fiu-Heng Lin, Hui-Ju Chiu, Shang-Ping Chen, Ted Chen, Anita Huang, Anthony W.H. Fong, Yi-Lin Chen, Yi-Fang Liu and C.S. Chang; without their efforts this book would not be possible. Finally, we wish to thank The Images Publishing Group Pty Ltd for preparing and publishing this book.

Index

Every effort has been made to trace the original source of copyright material contained in this book. The publishers would be pleased to hear from copyright holders to rectify any error or omissions.

The information and illustrations in this publication has been prepared and supplied by Haigo Shen & Partners, Architects & Engineers. While all reasonable efforts have been made to ensure accuracy, the publishers do not, under any circumstances, accept responsibility for errors, omissions and representations express or implied.